The Simply Kosher Cookbook

THE
Simply
KOSHER
Cookbook

100+ Recipes for Quick Weeknight Meals
and Easy Holiday Favorites

Nina Safar

PHOTOGRAPHY BY HÉLÈNE DUJARDIN

R
ROCKRIDGE
PRESS

For general information on our other products and services or to obtain technical support, please contact our Customer Care Department within the U.S. at (866) 744-2665, or outside the U.S. at (510) 253-0500.

Rockridge Press publishes its books in a variety of electronic and print formats. Some content that appears in print may not be available in electronic books, and vice versa.

TRADEMARKS: Rockridge Press and the Rockridge Press logo are trademarks or registered trademarks of Callisto Media Inc. and/or its affiliates, in the United States and other countries, and may not be used without written permission. All other trademarks are the property of their respective owners. Rockridge Press is not associated with any product or vendor mentioned in this book.

Interior and Cover Designer: Liz Cosgrove
Photo Art Director: Karen Beard
Editor: Bridget Fitzgerald
Production Editor: Edgar Doolan
Photography: © 2019 Hélène Dujardin
Food Styling: Anna Hampton
Author Photo: © Devorah Esakhan

ISBN: Print 978-1-64152-671-5
eBook 978-1-64152-672-2

This book is dedicated to the women in my life who have taught me that food is healing: My mother. Her mother, my bubbe. My sisters. My friends. They have all reminded me that there is no joy like sharing food with the people you love.

And to my mother I am most thankful.

I want to love like you do, laugh like you do, and fill my house with freshly baked goods like you do. You raised all 11 of us with joy and love and faith and cupcakes and frosting and laughter, and you did it without coffee. You celebrate life daily, and when I struggle I'm reminded to do the same. I love you and your sugar-loving, babka-baking, cheerleading heart.

STRAWBERRY FETA SALAD *page 16*

Contents

Introduction

FOOD IS MAGIC. The ability a single dish has to connect those gathered around it, eating it, creating moments remembered once the dish is long gone, is simply magical. Growing up in a large family of 11 children spanning different ages (with a 21-year gap between the oldest and youngest), it would have been so easy for us to get lost in the daily routine of work, school, and homework—if not for our nightly meals as a family. Without fail, when it was time for supper, we would take a time-out from deadlines, essay writing, and friends, and join together around the kitchen table for the chance to refuel and connect over delicious mouthfuls of my mother's food. Even as a young child I always looked forward to those precious moments together, full of happy—and loud—chatter. Now, I wish to establish those memories for my own children.

When I create a recipe, I have three things in mind: It has to be kosher, it hopefully tastes good, and it must be easy. You might be surprised to learn that I don't actually enjoy cooking all that much. I just really like serving—and eating!—good food. Less time spent in the kitchen means more time spent with my family and friends around the table. Those are the moments I cherish.

I am excited to share my favorite recipes with you right here: the food I actually cook for myself and my family on a weekly basis. Depending on my energy level (and who I want to impress), sometimes I might dress up a recipe, but most nights, my motto is "super simple and seriously tasty." Forget Pinterest-perfect composition: At the end of the day, all this hungry girl wants is a delicious and fuss-free dinner (with minimal dishes to wash!).

I learned how to cook by watching my mother, queen of quickly prepared tasty meals and delectable kid-friendly treats. There was always a warm home-cooked meal and some kind of yummy snack waiting for us after school. My mother's chocolate babka is still my favorite dessert, and I love the fact that

I can always count on there being freshly baked chocolate chip cookies in her cookie jar. When I was in high school, I would often cook dinner for my siblings, which is kind of where my love for easy cooking comes from. I had tests to prep for and work to do, so I couldn't exactly fuss around in the kitchen (especially cooking for 10 people). When I write a recipe, I like to strip it down to the essentials. What does it really need to taste good? Everything else is optional and can depend on how much energy I have left at the end of the day.

Whether you want to impress your future mother-in-law with a good potato kugel, cook an easy rush-hour dinner that your children will eat, or score points hosting a dinner party for friends, there is a recipe here for you just waiting to be cooked, eaten, and enjoyed with loved ones.

Chapter One

KOSHER MADE SIMPLE

Consider this chapter your cheat sheet for cooking kosher food. Kosher food is food that has been prepared according to a specific set of Jewish dietary laws that originate from the Torah. While the laws of *kashrut* (kosher observance) are intricate, they don't have to be overwhelming. This chapter will break them down for you, creating easy-to-use guidelines so you can feel confident preparing a kosher meal, no matter your skill level. From shopping for groceries (knowing which products to buy) and bringing them home to your kosher kitchen (no worries— there's a section to help you set that up) to cooking a delicious dinner that would make your bubbe proud, this book will be here to guide you along the way.

TRADITIONS

Growing up in an orthodox Jewish community in Brooklyn meant that Thursday night cholent and kugel crawls were the norm, and that we could easily find an assortment of different flavored herring at our local kosher supermarket. It wasn't until I started blogging at kosherinthekitch.com that I began receiving numerous questions from readers across the globe: *Does a rabbi have to bless the food in order for it to be kosher?* No, he does not. *If I cook kosher chicken in kosher cow's milk, is that okay?* While I love a good creamy chicken dish, it's not kosher to mix meat and dairy—however, swapping cow's milk for nondairy coconut milk or almond milk are both great alternative kosher options.

After answering dozens of these types of queries, I realized how overwhelming all of the kashrut rules can be—especially if you didn't grow up following them. The way I look at it, there are the laws of kosher, and then there is the spirit of kosher, which for me has always been about sharing food with loved ones both on joyous occasions and in times of need. I love taking the traditional recipes I learned as a child and bringing them into my own kitchen with a modern twist. Updating the classics (topping chicken pot pie with matzo balls, and turning my bubbe's recipe for challah into barbecue pastrami-stuffed challah, for instance) is a favorite challenge of mine. For me, kosher cooking is as much about joy as it is about rituals and guidelines.

With this cookbook, I hope to make it super simple for anyone and everyone to get in the kitchen and cook delicious kosher food. (Of course, if you're well past the introductory stage of your kosher kitchen education, just skip past this intro section to find tons of easy, tasty recipes to add to your repertoire.)

The Rules

The laws of kashrut are broken down according to what we can and cannot eat. In Judaism, we believe that anything can be sacred, including food, which is why we say a blessing before we eat, to make it holy. In order for approved foods to be holy, though, they must be prepared in certain ways.

Here are the basic guidelines:

1. The meats of most fowl, such as chickens, turkeys, ducks, and geese, and animals that chew their cud and have split hooves are kosher. Those

animals include cows, sheep, and goats. These animals can be eaten once they are slaughtered according to the laws of shehitah, which state that no additional pain should be inflicted on the animal during the process.

2. Milk produced from kosher animals and dairy products that use this milk are kosher.

3. Eggs from kosher animals are kosher (including caviar).

4. Kosher seafood includes fish that have *both* fins and removable scales (that means no shellfish and no bottom-feeders or scavengers, such as catfish).

5. All whole fruits and vegetables are kosher.

6. Meat and dairy cannot be cooked or eaten together in the same meal.

When shopping in the grocery store for meats, poultry, seafood, and anything that is packaged or processed—including wine and other beverages—ask to see proof of the kosher certification or check the labels. (See page 154 for a helpful guide featuring some of the more popular kosher symbols on packaged foods.) Though all whole, fresh produce is kosher, it should be noted that insects are not kosher, so before consuming fruits and vegetables, you should wash and check them to confirm that there are indeed no bugs. Certain vegetables such as broccoli, kale, and lettuce often have small bugs in the crevices and should be carefully checked before eating.

MODIFICATIONS

Often, people choose to make modifications to the laws of kashrut based on their lifestyles or personal preferences. Many keep kosher kitchens at home but are less strict when it comes to dining out, frequenting non-kosher certified restaurants and coffee shops and simply asking about ingredients to find dishes that might meet their standards. When I am traveling, I often look for strictly vegan restaurants if I'm somewhere without kosher options, as those restaurant kitchens are more likely to meet kosher standards. It's important to be familiar with the laws and understand why something may or may not be kosher. When in doubt, you can always ask your local orthodox rabbi.

Modern Kosher

The laws of kashrut might seem restrictive, but once you start following them, you'll find that keeping kosher can fit pretty easily within any diet or lifestyle—whether you follow a vegan, gluten-free, or sugar-free diet or enjoy cooking and eating farm-to-table foods. Many people often associate kosher cooking with high fat and greasy foods, but this couldn't be further from the truth—fresh leafy greens, ripe fruit, whole grains, and clean proteins are all fantastic parts of a healthy kosher diet. There is no current dietary trend that cannot be made kosher. Once you have the right kashrut-approved ingredients and master just a few simple tweaks and substitutions, you can pretty much cook anything.

For example, a classic chicken Alfredo is, of course, not kosher, as it combines meat and dairy. However, it was something I had always wanted to taste—it just looks so delicious! So I thought to myself, *How can I make this dish kosher?* I decided to make a vegan version of the classic white sauce by using nondairy

Entertaining in Your Kosher Home

To avoid any conflict between different kashrut standards, when you entertain, ask your guests to simply enjoy their time off from cooking and not feel pressured to bring anything. If one of your guests insists that they can't come empty-handed, offer some nonfood options: Flowers are always a lovely addition to the table, and an extra bottle of kosher wine is never a bad thing. In addition, if you are the guest and would like to gift your host with something that isn't related to any particular kind of food, try a more permanent contribution: I like to give my favorite serving bowls or a cute cutting board. Something that can be used for future entertaining is always a welcome change from the usual dessert or food options. They may not be able to break it out for that particular party, but you might see it next time you visit.

nut milk instead of cow's milk. Since the sauce was no longer dairy based, I was then able to add in slices of spiced grilled chicken—I had never tasted a rich cream sauce with chicken like that before, and it was such a simple swap (recipe on page 88). When you stop thinking of kosher as a restrictive diet and instead shift your attention to the bounty of ingredients you have to work with, the possibilities are plenty and tasty.

THE KOSHER KITCHEN

Welcome to the kosher kitchen. Since we don't mix meat and dairy foods, many kosher kitchens will have two sets of appliances and basic kitchen elements—such as two sets of dishes and utensils, two microwaves, and even two ovens and two sinks. But of course, this isn't always possible, and not all things have to be doubled even in a strict kosher kitchen. For example, if you have a small kitchen, you can use your oven for meat or dairy (depending on what you cook more often) and then use a separate convection oven on your countertop for the other. I have always cooked in a small kitchen. My very first apartment in Brooklyn had no counter space at all, so I had to build my own prep area. I had one tiny oven, which I chose to use for meat because I cook chicken for dinner a lot throughout the week, and I used a small convection oven (on my makeshift countertop) for cooking dairy foods such as baked ziti, pizza, cheesecake, and anything else with cheese or milk. Growing up, my mom's kitchen had a similar setup (gotta love small Brooklyn kitchens), so I knew it could be done.

To Each Their Own

Not all kosher kitchens look the same, which is why it is so important to learn the basic rules and guidelines of kashrut and then decide how you want to apply them to your daily life. The idea is to make them work in your own home and kitchen. If you are setting up a kosher kitchen for the first time and feel overwhelmed by all this information, just take a breath and relax. It all boils down to two basic rules:

1. Start off with kosher products

2. Don't mix meat and dairy

To avoid mixing meat and dairy, it's a good idea to have separate prep tools for each type of meal—knives, cutting boards, spatulas, etc. I like to buy utensils in separate colors for meat and dairy so there is no confusion in the kitchen. For example, a red spatula for meat and a blue spatula for dairy. True, the ideal kosher kitchen has two of every single thing used for food prep and cooking (in a truly ideal world, there would be a private chef in there as well!)—but most kitchens don't have that kind of space, and many households simply don't have the budget to purchase double of everything. So while that might be the dream kosher kitchen, it doesn't have to be yours. I love my vintage yellow KitchenAid® stand mixer, but I'm not buying two of them! So I keep it pareve, and I have a separate, less expensive, and much smaller hand mixer for when I want to mix things that contain dairy.

Pantry and Fridge Staples

Certain staples are a must-have in my home kitchen; these are products that allow me to prepare quick and easy dinners without having to schlep to the grocery store. (I'm the hostess who likes to score points in the kitchen without sweating for it!) While I like to buy my proteins fresh, boxed and canned items like pasta, quinoa, rice, beans, chickpeas, and jars of basil marinara sauce are all great to have on hand for easy cooking. I don't like purchasing ingredients that will only be used once or maybe twice before they expire. I hate waste, and also, I'd rather spend that money on my morning latte! I like to stock my kitchen with items that can be used in multiple recipes and will help me get dinner on the table in a short amount of time. Here are a few favorites I always have in my kitchen:

Coconut milk   I always have a few cans of coconut milk in my pantry (or refrigerator), as it is fantastic for making creamy nondairy dishes and desserts. It is especially delicious in Cinnamon Coconut Whipped Cream (page 27) and Butternut Squash Quinoa Stew (page 94).

Almond milk and soy milk   Similar to coconut milk, I use almond milk and soy milk as nondairy options when recipes call for dairy elements or binders. I add them to sauces for chicken, and use them to make pareve desserts that can be served with meat-based meals.

Nondairy spread   Earth Balance is my preferred butter substitute for cooking and baking. It's basically a healthier margarine and is great when you want to whip up a nondairy buttercream or roux.

Pasta, quinoa, and rice   These are all classic must-haves to stock up on, and since they are pareve, they can be paired with any dinner (always a win in a kosher kitchen).

Honey   Honey is my favorite sweetener for marinades and dressings.

Chickpeas and tahini   I love knowing that I can make my own hummus with these two simple ingredients. It's tastier than the store-bought versions, so easy to prepare, and it makes a great addition to any meal. You can serve it with shakshuka for brunch (page 86), as a side with a meat dinner, or keep it vegan by serving it with roasted veggies.

Vegetable stock   While chicken stock is usually the pantry standard, I like to keep vegetable stock on hand so I can use it in both meat and dairy recipes.

Marinara sauce   Find a brand and flavor of sauce that you like, and keep a few jars on hand for lazy meatballs and a quick start to shakshuka. When the final dish tastes good, no one cares that it started from a jar.

Frozen garlic cubes   These are cubes of frozen chopped garlic that can be found in your local supermarket's freezer section. When you are short on time, having access to already-prepped garlic that you can toss straight in the pan is a lifesaver. You will thank me later.

Frozen dill, basil, and cilantro   While I love fresh herbs, I find that store-bought bunches are often too large and end up going to waste in my refrigerator. Thankfully, most grocery stores now sell cubes of minced herbs in their freezer sections, usually near the frozen garlic. They are always good to have in your freezer to add to any dressing, marinade, or sauce.

Frozen piecrusts   Your guests will always leave happy if you serve dessert. My go-to treat for entertaining is crumble, and it's always a hit (see page 131 for the recipe).

Frozen fruit   Strawberries, raspberries, blueberries, and anything else that can be added to cobblers or smoothies are good to have on hand.

Keeping Equipment Simple

If I have room on my counter, I want to use it for cookies, not extra kitchen gadgets. When I'm thinking about making a purchase for the kitchen, I like to ask myself if it's something that I will use daily. If not, it's a no-go for me. I'm super basic with my gadgets. All I really need is a good cutting board (one that won't slide on the counter), a reliable knife (that will cut through anything), a good peeler (don't underestimate how frustrating it is to peel veggies and fruit with a bad one), a grill pan, a large skillet or frying pan, a soup pot, and a smaller skillet. I have two of each of these tools—one for meat and one for dairy—with the exception of the grill pan, since that is used only for meat.

The only large appliances I suggest making room for are a stand mixer (super helpful for making challah and all desserts), a slow cooker, and a pressure cooker.

You don't need a super-size kitchen when keeping kosher—you just need to be smart about what you stock in the kitchen you have. Stick to the basics and don't buy anything that won't be used weekly. Yes, I would love to own an ice cream sandwich maker, but in reality, will I use it enough? Probably not. So for now it's staying on my wish list and not in my cabinet.

Keeping Things Organized

Keep your kitchen organized with designated drawers and cabinets for separate meat and dairy tools, appliances, dishes, and utensils. You can even place convenient meat, dairy, and pareve stickers on the items in your kitchen so guests will know where they can get their cereal bowls, which mug they can grab for coffee, or which drawer holds the steak knives. It also helps if you color coordinate (for instance, red utensils and equipment for meat, blue for dairy), as the visual cue will keep you from absentmindedly mixing dairy and meat cutlery and other items.

Two of This, One of That

 I like to own two of all the basics—anything that will come into direct contact with what I am cooking—to avoid confusion and prevent the accidental mixing of meat and dairy items. That means cutting boards, knives, pots and pans, spatulas, and serving dishes. While peelers are most often used for fruits and veggies, I still suggest having two, since they are small, easy to store, and inexpensive. Items such as can openers can be kept pareve, depending on what you are using them for. However, if you like to cook with condensed milk or other canned dairy items, it might be a good idea to have separate can openers. Please note that these are all merely suggestions, and while they may work for me and my kitchen, only you will be able to decide what works best for yours.

I have a separate drawer in my kitchen where I store pareve items that are not used for meat or dairy (such as an egg slicer, cookie cutters, mini spatulas used to scoop things out of jars, and a rolling pin for dough). Those are just a few examples of items that you don't necessarily need two of. When purchasing a new utensil that is made of metal or glass, you can make it kosher by immersing it in a *mikvah*, a pool or well of natural water (your local synagogue should have one or know where to locate one), and reciting a blessing. This process is called *toveling*.

ABOUT THE RECIPES

There is nothing like a good home-cooked meal to bring people together, but you don't have to be a chef to make it happen. Here's the thing—I don't actually *like* big, fancy cooking. Spending a long time in the kitchen waiting for a dish to finally be ready to eat is not something I find enjoyable. But preparing a quick and tasty meal and then savoring that meal with loved ones? Now that's something I love. Each dish in this cookbook is deliciously simple with minimal ingredients and prep and maximum flavor.

The Chapters

The recipes in this book are divided by strategy instead of by meal: You can choose your dish based on how much time you have to cook, how many ingredients you have on hand, or which method you want to use. The recipes in chapter four (page 53) are all limited to five ingredients (not counting salt, pepper, and oil). Not in the mood for multiple dishes to wash? No problem. You can cook a savory meal of chicken and rice with spinach and only have one pot to clean (page 75). Chapter six (page 93) is dedicated to the magic of our favorite kitchen appliances, the slow cooker and the pressure cooker. (Note that I tested my recipes using a 8-quart Instant Pot®, but you can adapt them for your electric pressure cooker.) Trying to get your kids to eat dinner, and fast? Make lazy meatballs that even the pickiest eater will devour (page 60). Feeling like a low-energy hostess but still want to score points in the kitchen? Bake up my one-bowl Chocolate Chip Zucchini Walnut Muffins (page 110)—and make it a double batch, because everyone will want seconds. To navigate the book by meat, dairy, or pareve dishes, see the index on page 157.

The Tips

You'll see tips at the bottom of some of the recipes that offer more information, helpful cooking tricks and variations, or time-saving hacks:

Make-ahead Tip: Helpful info on what can be done or prepped in advance.

Ingredient Tip: More info on selecting and working with ingredients.

Variation Tip: Suggestions for adding or changing ingredients to mix things up a little or try something new with the recipe.

The Ingredients

You don't need to have access to a specialty kosher grocery store to make the dishes in this book—all of the ingredients can be found at your local supermarket. As a single mom, I don't have the budget or time for anything expensive or complicated, but as a food lover, I need a result that is delicious. I often use ready-made ingredients if it helps make the process quicker and tastes just as good. Frozen vegetables and piecrusts and jars of premade pasta sauce, for example, are fantastic ways to save both time and money in the kitchen. When everyone is licking their plate clean, they're not asking if the sauce was homemade. They just want more of it.

CLASSIC HUMMUS *page 14*

Chapter Two
NO-COOK

Classic Hummus

P PAREVE ✦ EASY PREP **GF** GRAIN FREE **V** VEGAN

MAKES ABOUT 2 CUPS (SERVES 8 TO 10) | PREP TIME: 10 MINUTES

When it comes to sandwich spreads, I'm team hummus over mayonnaise all the way. Hummus is super simple to make from scratch, and the homemade version *always* tastes better than any store-bought container. You can easily create your own flavor variations, too (see Variation Tip). I love this creamy, rich hummus slathered on crunchy toasted bread, or as a dip with sliced carrot or roasted cauliflower—but my favorite way to eat it is on a fresh pita, one big bite at a time.

2 tablespoons tahini

2 garlic cloves, peeled

Juice of 1 lemon

2 tablespoons cold water

¼ cup olive oil (plus additional for serving)

¼ teaspoon fine sea salt

½ teaspoon ground cumin

2 (15-ounce) cans chickpeas (garbanzo beans), rinsed and drained

1 teaspoon za'atar spice blend, for serving

1 teaspoon sesame seeds, for serving

1. In the bowl of a food processor, combine the tahini, garlic cloves, lemon juice, water, olive oil, sea salt, and ground cumin; process until smooth.

2. Add the chickpeas and purée until they are completely broken down and the hummus reaches your desired consistency.

3. Serve drizzled with olive oil and sprinkled with the za'atar and sesame seeds.

Variation Tip: You can easily create flavored hummus by adding ingredients to the hummus base—try chopped roasted beets, roasted red peppers, extra garlic cloves, or hot sauce. For spinach-artichoke hummus, add ¼ cup baby spinach leaves and ¼ cup jarred marinated artichokes. Additionally, you can top hummus with savory toppings such as spiced ground beef, thinly sliced grilled chicken, or even Shakshuka (page 86).

Per serving: Calories: 182; Total fat: 10g; Total carbs: 18g; Fiber: 5g; Sugar: 3g; Protein: 6g; Sodium: 69mg

Shredded Kale Salad with Creamy Tahini Dressing

(P) **PAREVE** (GF) **GRAIN FREE** ⊛ **EASY PREP** (V) **VEGETARIAN**

SERVES 4 | PREP TIME: 10 MINUTES

Kale, carrots, purple cabbage, and chickpeas create a vibrant, crunchy salad base, while tahini and honey blend together to form the perfect creamy (yet nondairy!) dressing. Combine the ingredients in a large bowl or serve them lined up on a platter for a colorful dish everyone will want to dig into. You can make this a more filling meal by adding some protein, such as sliced hardboiled eggs, grilled chicken, or cubed tofu (see Variation Tip for more).

¼ cup tahini

¼ cup water

Juice of 1 lemon

4 cups shredded kale or romaine leaves

1 cup peeled and shredded carrots

1 cup shredded purple cabbage

1 cup canned chickpeas (garbanzo beans), rinsed and drained

1 tablespoon honey

1 tablespoon red wine vinegar

2 tablespoons dried cranberries

1. In a small bowl, whisk together the tahini, water, and lemon juice.

2. Place the kale, carrots, purple cabbage, and chickpeas in a large salad bowl and drizzle the tahini mixture over the top. Add the honey and red wine vinegar to the salad bowl and mix well. Top with the dried cranberries before serving.

Variation Tip: Other protein items that upgrade this dish from a side or appetizer to the main meal include juicy chopped grilled chicken, flaked baked salmon, or avocado slices. Or add crumbled feta to make it a dairy meal.

Per serving: Calories: 251; Total fat: 9g; Total carbs: 38g; Fiber: 7g; Sugar: 12g; Protein: 8g; Sodium: 250mg

Strawberry Feta Salad

 DAIRY EASY PREP GF GRAIN FREE V VEGETARIAN

SERVES 5 TO 6 | PREP TIME: 10 MINUTES

When hosting, people often fuss so much about the main dish that they forget the power of a really great salad. This sweet and tasty combo of spinach, crumbled feta, and strawberries is a favorite of mine. With crunchy pecans and a sweet, flavorful dressing, it is sure to be a crowd pleaser.

6 ounces baby spinach

1 cup sliced strawberries

½ cup pecans

¼ cup crumbled feta

2 tablespoons balsamic vinegar

2 tablespoons olive oil

1 tablespoon brown sugar

1. Place the spinach in a large serving bowl. Layer the sliced strawberries, pecans, and crumbled feta on top.

2. In a small bowl, whisk together the balsamic vinegar, olive oil, and brown sugar.

3. Drizzle the dressing over the salad, toss, and serve.

Per serving: Calories: 171; Total fat: 15g; Total carbs: 7g; Fiber: 3g; Sugar: 4g; Protein: 3g; Sodium: 112mg

Flatbread Salad

 PAREVE   FAMILY FAVORITE  NUT FREE V VEGETARIAN

SERVES 5 TO 6 | PREP TIME: 10 MINUTES

It's not a Shabbat meal without some version of this cracker salad. This is one bowl that is always easy to clean after the meal since there is never anything left in it. (Seriously—I have never had leftovers of this dish. Not even a lone tomato or leaf of lettuce. It's all gone!) I love serving this alongside Fried Gefilte Fish Patties (page 66) and Hummus (page 14) and watching everyone chat around the table while enjoying the food I prepared in honor of Shabbat.

½ cup mayonnaise

¾ cup olive oil

1 teaspoon yellow mustard

2 tablespoons sugar (or 1 tablespoon honey)

¾ teaspoon salt

½ teaspoon freshly squeezed lemon juice

¾ teaspoon soy sauce

1 (8-ounce) bag romaine lettuce, torn

1 (16-ounce) bag shredded purple cabbage

1 red onion, thinly sliced

1 pound grape tomatoes, halved

1 (5-ounce) box flatbread crackers, crushed

1. In a small bowl, whisk together the mayonnaise, olive oil, yellow mustard, sugar, salt, lemon juice, and soy sauce.

2. In a large serving bowl, combine the romaine, cabbage, onion, and tomatoes and top with the crushed crackers.

3. Pour the dressing over the salad and toss well before serving.

Per serving: Calories: 591; Total fat: 50g; Total carbs: 34g; Fiber: 6g; Sugar: 12g; Protein: 5g; Sodium: 684mg

Mango Corn Salad

P PAREVE G GLUTEN FREE GF GRAIN FREE NUT FREE SF SUGAR FREE V VEGAN

SERVES 5 TO 6 | PREP TIME: 5 MINUTES

This zesty mango and corn salad with fresh lime juice and chopped cilantro is so refreshing and delicious. I tried it once at my friend Miera's house, and I have been enjoying it ever since. It has everything I want in a recipe: It's quick and easy to prep, and delicious enough to eat straight from the bowl. Of course, it also tastes fantastic in tacos, over a rice bowl with slices of grilled chicken, or bulked up with some sliced avocado and crumbled feta.

1 (15-ounce) can whole-kernel corn

1 large bunch cilantro, chopped

1 small red onion, diced

1 mango, peeled, pitted, and cubed

Juice of 1 lime

Combine the corn, cilantro, red onion, and mango in a large serving bowl. Squeeze the lime juice over the top and mix well.

Ingredient Tip: If you don't like the taste of cilantro, we can't be friends. Just kidding! I know many people don't enjoy the flavor, and for them I always recommend swapping in chopped fresh basil instead.

Per serving: Calories: 111; Total fat: 1g; Total carbs: 25g; Fiber: 3g; Sugar: 13g; Protein: 3g; Sodium: 235mg

Cranberry Sauce

P PAREVE ♥ FAMILY FAVORITE GF GRAIN FREE V VEGAN

MAKES ABOUT 2 CUPS (SERVES 6 TO 8) | PREP TIME: 5 MINUTES

This recipe is a family favorite from my sister-in-law, Sarrit, and makes a deliciously sweet addition to any holiday menu. My Thanksgiving meal would not be complete without a plate of sliced turkey covered in gravy, mashed potatoes, stuffing, and a serving of this cranberry sauce. The candied walnuts add a nice subtle crunch to the sweet and tart cranberry mixture and it always goes fast with my family. I like this sauce so much that I usually reserve a portion of it so I can have leftovers the day after Thanksgiving!

1 (16-ounce) can whole cranberry sauce

1 (11-ounce) can mandarin orange segments

1 (8-ounce) can crushed pineapple

1 cup candied walnuts

In a medium bowl, stir together the cranberry sauce, mandarin orange segments, crushed pineapple, and walnuts.

Make-ahead Tip: This recipe can be prepped in advance (without the walnuts) and stored in an airtight container in the refrigerator for several days. Just stir in the walnuts right before serving so they retain their crunch.

Per serving: Calories: 230; Total fat: 8g; Total carbs: 39g; Fiber: 3g; Sugar: 28g; Protein: 2g; Sodium: 53mg

Zesty Peach Salsa

P PAREVE **G** GLUTEN FREE **GF** GRAIN FREE **⊘** NUT FREE **SF** SUGAR FREE **V** VEGAN

MAKES ABOUT 2 CUPS (SERVES 6 TO 8) | PREP TIME: 10 MINUTES

With fresh lime juice and ripe peaches and tomatoes, this salsa is a standout—on its own or served with any number of dishes. I really enjoy it over a simple spiced salmon, alongside grilled chicken, or as a topping for tacos or rice bowls. While the ingredients are simple, the flavor is super vibrant and can be paired with many different foods. I like keeping a container of this salsa in my refrigerator so I always have it ready to go for whatever meal I'm serving.

5 peaches, peeled and diced

4 medium vine-ripened tomatoes, diced

2 tablespoons chopped fresh cilantro

1 small red onion, diced

Juice of 2 limes

In a medium bowl, combine the peaches, tomatoes, cilantro, red onion, and lime juice and mix well.

Per serving: Calories: 72; Total fat: 1g; Total carbs: 17g; Fiber: 3g; Sugar: 14g; Protein: 2g; Sodium: 5mg

Strawberry Basil Salsa

P PAREVE G GLUTEN FREE GF GRAIN FREE NUT FREE SF SUGAR FREE V VEGAN

MAKES ABOUT 2 CUPS (SERVES 8 TO 10) | PREP TIME: 10 MINUTES

By now you are probably aware of my love for a good salsa. I really enjoy how easy it is to prepare and the fact that you can have fun playing around with ingredients to create any flavor combo you want. I like to add this particular salsa to breakfast burritos with scrambled eggs and avocado or spoon it into wraps with turkey and lettuce. It also pairs especially well with grilled chicken, and can make a plain chicken breast feel like a gourmet meal in an instant.

1 pint strawberries, hulled and diced

1 small red onion, diced

1 avocado, pitted and diced

Juice of 1 lime

Leaves from 1 small bunch basil, chopped

Combine the strawberries, red onion, avocado, lime juice, and basil in a medium bowl; mix well.

Variation Tip: Up the ante by adding a splash of store-bought balsamic glaze to the salsa and pair it with salmon or chicken. It creates an additional depth of flavor.

Per serving: Calories: 56; Total fat: 4g; Total carbs: 7g; Fiber: 3g; Sugar: 3g; Protein: 1g; Sodium: 3mg

Asian Coleslaw Salad

 PAREVE V VEGAN

SERVES 4 TO 6 | PREP TIME: 10 MINUTES

There is no greater joy than finding a friend—especially one who enjoys food as much as you do. My friend Dini Goldman shares my love for eating good food and is always just a voice note away to discuss new recipes or holiday menu ideas. This is her salad recipe, a crunchy sweet blend of coleslaw veggies, sesame seeds, sunflower seeds, and sliced almonds topped with an apple cider vinegar dressing and garnished with crunchy chow mein noodles. It's a delicious, easy side and can even be turned into the main dish by adding slices of grilled chicken.

1 (14-ounce) bag coleslaw mix

2 scallions, chopped

¼ cup sliced almonds

¼ cup sesame seeds

¼ cup sunflower seeds

¼ cup packed brown sugar

6 tablespoons apple cider vinegar

½ cup olive oil

½ teaspoon salt

¼ teaspoon freshly ground black pepper

1 cup chow mein noodles, for garnish

1. In a large serving bowl, combine the coleslaw mix, scallions, almonds, sesame seeds, and sunflower seeds.

2. In a medium mixing bowl, whisk together the brown sugar, apple cider vinegar, olive oil, salt, and pepper.

3. Pour the dressing over the coleslaw mix, toss well, and garnish with the noodles.

Ingredient Tip: You can toast the nuts and seeds for added flavor by placing them on a baking sheet and baking them at 350°F for 8 to 10 minutes until lightly browned. Once toasted, store the nuts and seeds in an airtight container in the refrigerator for up to 1 year.

Make-ahead Tip: The salad can be prepped and dressed in advance; just wait to add the chow mein noodles until right before serving.

Per serving: Calories: 495; Total fat: 40g; Total carbs: 33g; Fiber: 4g; Sugar: 9g; Protein: 6g; Sodium: 369mg

Easy Mimosas

P PAREVE **G** GLUTEN FREE **GF** GRAIN FREE **⬭** NUT FREE **V** VEGAN

SERVES 5 TO 6 | PREP TIME: 5 MINUTES

As I always say, tipsy guests are happy guests—they are happy to eat anything, and that takes the pressure off hosting! So my trick is to start any meal I host with a good beverage. This is my lazy girl's mimosa, since it's simply a combination of Moscato wine and orange juice (you can't mess it up and it always tastes good). You can have fun with different garnishes by adding fresh mint leaves or rosemary stems, or tucking orange slices or strawberries into each serving glass.

Ice cubes

1 (750-milliliter) bottle Moscato (or any sweet white wine)

3 cups chilled orange juice

Orange slices, for garnish

Fresh mint leaves, for garnish

1. Fill 5 or 6 serving glasses with ice.

2. Fill the glasses about halfway with Moscato, then top them off with the orange juice.

3. Garnish with orange slices and mint leaves and serve.

Make-ahead Tip: You can make mimosa ice cubes by freezing the recipe in ice cube molds and adding them to the serving glass in place of regular ice. This prevents drinks from becoming diluted—and looks really pretty when on display!

Per serving: Calories: 298; Total fat: 0g; Total carbs: 35g; Fiber: 0g; Sugar: 24g; Protein: 1g; Sodium: 14mg

Blackberry Pomegranate Spritzer

P PAREVE   **G** GLUTEN FREE   **GF** GRAIN FREE   **◇** NUT FREE   **V** VEGAN

SERVES 4 | PREP TIME: 10 MINUTES

These nonalcoholic, sweet, and bold-tasting spritzers are perfect for both adults and children. (But if you really want to start the meal off with a buzz, add a small splash of vodka for adults only before serving.) To make them feel extra fancy, garnish each serving glass with blackberries and fresh slices of lemon or lime.

Ice cubes

1 cup pomegranate juice

1 (1-liter) bottle carbonated water

1 cup blackberries, for garnish

Lime or lemon slices, for garnish

1. Fill 4 serving glasses with ice.

2. Pour 2 tablespoons of pomegranate juice into each serving glass, then top them off with carbonated water.

3. Add several blackberries to each serving glass and garnish with a lemon or lime slice.

Variation Tip: Swap out plain carbonated water for flavored seltzer, such as lime or berry. You can also add fresh herbs, such as mint or rosemary, to each glass for a fragrant garnish.

Per serving: Calories: 53; Total fat: 0g; Total carbs: 13g; Fiber: 2g; Sugar: 10g; Protein: 1g; Sodium: 5mg

Pumpkin Spiced Cheesecake Mousse

 DAIRY GLUTEN FREE GF GRAIN FREE NUT FREE OPTION

MAKES 25 SHOT GLASSES | PREP TIME: 15 MINUTES

Pumpkin spice is a fall favorite for a reason, and this pumpkin spiced mousse—with its creamy texture and rich flavor—is a reminder that it is indeed the most wonderful time of the year. The individual-size portions make for easy serving and cleanup. I enjoy serving this dessert for breakfast on Shabbat (it's a family tradition to eat baked goods such as cake and cupcakes or cheesecake to celebrate the holy Shabbat) or any time when entertaining over the holidays. If you don't have shot glasses, this recipe also can be served in 14 six-ounce bowls, using an ice cream scoop to portion the mousse and a cookie dough scoop to top with whipped cream. To go nut free, omit the pecans and sprinkle with ground cinnamon.

2 cups chilled heavy whipping cream

8 ounces cream cheese, at room temperature

1 cup canned pumpkin purée

½ teaspoon ground cinnamon

¼ teaspoon ground ginger

¼ teaspoon ground cloves

¼ teaspoon ground nutmeg

½ teaspoon vanilla extract

1 cup plus 2 tablespoons powdered sugar, divided

Candied pecans, for serving (optional)

1. Chill a metal mixing bowl and whisk in the freezer for at least 10 minutes.

2. Pour the cream into the chilled bowl and, using the chilled whisk, whip it until soft peaks have formed; set aside.

3. In a separate large bowl, stir together the cream cheese, pumpkin purée, cinnamon, ginger, cloves, nutmeg, and vanilla. Add 1 cup of the powdered sugar and mix well.

4. Fold half of the whipped cream into the pumpkin-cream cheese mixture and mix gently until just combined. Mix the remaining 2 tablespoons of powdered sugar into the remaining whipped cream.

5. Serve the pumpkin mousse in shot glasses topped with the sweetened whipped cream and candied pecans (if using).

Per serving (1 shot glass): Calories: 87; Total fat: 7g; Total carbs: 6g; Fiber: 0g; Sugar: 5g; Protein: 1g; Sodium: 31mg

Dark Chocolate Pomegranate Bark

P PAREVE **G** GLUTEN FREE **GF** GRAIN FREE **⊘** NUT FREE **V** VEGAN

SERVES 5 TO 6 | PREP TIME: 10 MINUTES

I love a dessert that is easy to prep and is always a crowd pleaser! This is vegan, so it can be served with any meal (meat or dairy)—and it's even good for you! Bittersweet chocolate is rich in antioxidants, as are pomegranate arils, the juicy pods that house the fruit's tiny white seeds. To avoid the hassle of removing the arils yourself, you can buy them packaged in a container at the supermarket. They add a surprising crunch and wonderful pop of color, plus an extra boost of nutrients.

10 ounces bittersweet dark chocolate, chopped

1 cup pomegranate arils, divided

Per serving: Calories: 381; Total fat: 19g; Total carbs: 48g; Fiber: 7g; Sugar: 40g; Protein: 4g; Sodium: 3mg

1. Line a large baking sheet with parchment paper.

2. Place the chocolate in a microwave-safe dish and heat it in the microwave in 30-second increments, stirring in between, until smooth and completely melted. Stir in half of the pomegranate arils.

3. Pour the chocolate-pomegranate mixture onto the prepared baking sheet, using a spatula to smooth it out evenly to a ¼-inch thickness. Top with the remaining pomegranate arils, gently pressing them down into the chocolate.

4. Refrigerate for about 30 minutes or until the chocolate has hardened. Using a knife or your hands, break the hardened chocolate into pieces.

5. Store the chocolate bark in a plastic zip-top bag or airtight container in the refrigerator for up to 1 week.

Variation Tip: Season melted chocolate with sea salt, ground ginger, or a dash of cayenne pepper for a nice kick of flavor! You can also top the melted chocolate with different ingredients such as crushed pretzels, candied ginger, chopped-up candy and chocolate bars, dried fruits and nuts, cereal, or a drizzle of caramel.

Cinnamon Coconut Whipped Cream

P PAREVE **G** GLUTEN FREE **GF** GRAIN FREE **⊗** NUT FREE **V** VEGAN

MAKES ABOUT 1 CUP (SERVES 6) | PREP TIME: 10 MINUTES, PLUS OVERNIGHT TO CHILL

No dessert is complete without a serving of sweet whipped cream layered on top in soft peaks. Whether it's a chocolate fudge brownie warm from the oven, or a bowl full of deliciously ripe sliced fruit, a dollop of whipped cream is the perfect finishing touch. This super simple vegan version can be served after a meat meal, since it's made from coconut milk. It has the same texture as a classic whipped cream, with a slight coconut flavor that prevents it from being overly sweet—but if you're not a fan of coconut, you can simply add more powdered sugar and cinnamon to the base to further mellow the flavor.

1 (13.5-ounce) can full-fat coconut milk, chilled overnight in the refrigerator

3 tablespoons powdered sugar

1 teaspoon vanilla extract

¼ teaspoon ground cinnamon

1. Place the metal bowl of an electric mixer and the whisk attachment or beaters in the freezer for at least 10 minutes.

2. Open the can of chilled coconut milk and, using a spoon, scoop out the solid coconut cream at the top. (Don't throw out the coconut water; you can use it for a smoothie later on!) Place the coconut cream in the chilled bowl and beat it with the chilled whisk attachment or beaters until soft peaks form. Add the powdered sugar, vanilla, and cinnamon, and beat until just combined. Serve immediately.

Make-ahead Tip: Once you taste this whipped cream, you will understand the need to keep your refrigerator stocked with at least a few cans of coconut milk. That way, you can easily prepare this treat without having to wait for the coconut milk to chill. You can also whip the cream in advance and store it in the refrigerator in an airtight container; simply whip it once more before serving.

Per serving: Calories: 108; Total fat: 4g; Total carbs: 18g; Fiber: 0g; Sugar: 17g; Protein: 0g; Sodium: 9mg

QUINOA SALAD WITH AVOCADO AND POMEGRANATE SEEDS *page 35*

Chapter Three
30 MINUTES

Fluffy Lemon Blueberry Pancakes

DAIRY ● **FAMILY FAVORITE** ● **NUT FREE**

SERVES 6 TO 8 | **PREP TIME: 5 MINUTES** | **COOK TIME: 15 MINUTES**

Growing up, Sunday mornings always started off with a plate piled high with fresh pancakes. My siblings and I would gather around the breakfast table for bites of these soft, fluffy little cakes that melted in our mouths. We would giggle and fight over the syrup as we talked about the week ahead. I updated my childhood favorite by adding some fresh lemon zest and tart blueberries to the batter. Now, when I bake a batch for my boys, my heart is filled with the warm fuzzies of nostalgia.

2 cups all-purpose flour

¼ cup sugar

1 teaspoon salt

3 teaspoons baking powder

1¾ cups milk (dairy milk or any nondairy nut milk)

2 eggs

¼ cup canola oil

Zest of 1 lemon

1½ cups fresh blueberries

Nonstick cooking spray

Maple syrup, fruit, powdered sugar, and/or whipped cream, for serving (optional)

1. In a large mixing bowl, combine the flour, sugar, salt, and baking powder. Mix in the milk, eggs, and oil until well combined and smooth. Add in the lemon zest and blueberries and stir together until combined.

2. Heat a large skillet over medium heat and coat it with nonstick cooking spray.

3. Scoop ¼-cup mounds of the pancake batter onto the skillet (an ice cream scoop works great), spacing them about 1 inch apart. When bubbles appear on top, flip the pancakes over to cook the other side. Cook until both sides are golden brown. Repeat with the remaining batter.

4. Serve hot with the toppings of your choice.

Variation Tip: This recipe is surprisingly adaptable for various dietary needs. For more fiber, swap out the all-purpose flour for whole-wheat flour. To make pareve pancakes, simply substitute any nondairy milk for the cow's milk. You can also make them vegan by replacing the eggs with 6 tablespoons water whisked with 2 tablespoons ground flaxseed meal.

Per serving: Calories: 342; Total fat: 13g; Total carbs: 50g; Fiber: 2g; Sugar: 15g; Protein: 9g; Sodium: 445mg

Pumpkin Pie Pancakes

 DAIRY ⊘ NUT FREE

SERVES 6 TO 8 | **PREP TIME: 10 MINUTES** | **COOK TIME: 15 MINUTES**

Savor the flavors of fall (and, of course, pumpkin spice!) with these deliciously festive pancakes. Soft, cakelike, and served with whipped cream, they'll make you think you're eating pumpkin pie for breakfast. There is nothing better than waking up on a lazy fall or winter Sunday morning and digging into a pile of these treats. If you host guests for Thanksgiving weekend, greet them in the morning with a plate of these and they will be *extra* thankful.

2 cups all-purpose flour

6 tablespoons sugar

3 teaspoons
baking powder

1 teaspoon salt

1¾ cups milk

2 eggs

1½ cups canned
pumpkin purée

½ teaspoon ground
cinnamon

½ teaspoon
ground ginger

½ teaspoon
ground nutmeg

½ teaspoon
ground cloves

Nonstick cooking spray

Whipped cream, maple
syrup, and candied
pecans, for serving
(optional)

1. In a large mixing bowl, combine the flour, sugar, baking powder and salt. Mix in the milk and eggs until well combined and smooth. Add the pumpkin purée, cinnamon, ginger, nutmeg, and cloves. Mix well.

2. Heat a large skillet over medium heat and coat it with nonstick cooking spray.

3. Scoop ¼-cup mounds of the pancake batter onto the skillet (an ice cream scoop works great), spacing them about 1 inch apart. When bubbles appear on top, flip the pancakes over to cook the other side. Cook until both sides are golden brown. Repeat with the remaining batter.

4. Serve hot with the toppings of your choice.

Make-ahead Tip: Make a double batch of these pancakes and store half of them in the freezer for quick, heat-and-eat breakfasts (or treats). Store them in airtight zip-top bags in the freezer for up to 3 months.

Per serving: Calories: 282; Total fat: 4g; Total carbs: 54g; Fiber: 3g; Sugar: 18g; Protein: 9g; Sodium: 448mg

Classic Waffles

 DAIRY FAMILY FAVORITE ⬡ NUT FREE

SERVES 4 TO 5 | PREP TIME: 5 MINUTES | COOK TIME: 15 MINUTES

My favorite meal to host is brunch. With a giant pitcher of my Easy Mimosas (page 23) and a batch of fresh-from-the-griddle waffles topped with whipped cream and berries, I am a happy hostess. This recipe (from my sister Tova) cooks up thick, restaurant-quality waffles that you can enjoy in the comfort of your own home—because brunch, no matter how fancy, is so much better in pajamas.

2 eggs

2 cups white whole-wheat flour

1¾ cups milk

¼ cup canola oil

¼ teaspoon salt

½ teaspoon vanilla extract

Pinch ground cinnamon

6 tablespoons sugar

1 tablespoon flaxseed meal

Powdered sugar, whipped cream, chopped fresh fruit, and/or maple syrup, for serving (optional)

1. In a large mixing bowl, whisk together the eggs, flour, milk, oil, salt, vanilla, cinnamon, sugar, and flaxseed.

2. Spoon the batter onto the waffle maker and cook until golden brown, according to the manufacturer's instructions.

3. Serve with your toppings of choice.

Per serving: Calories: 492; Total fat: 20g; Total carbs: 68g; Fiber: 8g; Sugar: 24g; Protein: 14g; Sodium: 229mg

Sweet Noodle Kugel Muffins

 PAREVE   NUT FRE    VEGETARIAN

MAKES 12 MUFFINS | PREP TIME: 5 MINUTES | COOK TIME: 25 MINUTES

Some recipes simply remind you of home. One bite of these sweet noodle kugel muffins and I'm back in Brooklyn, sitting in my mom's kitchen watching her prep for Shabbat. While the sweet cinnamon-laced noodles almost taste like dessert, tradition has me serving them alongside chicken and potato kugel during the Shabbat meal. My mother cooks this recipe as one large kugel in a 9-by-13-inch baking dish; however, I like the individual-size portions you get from a muffin tin.

Nonstick cooking spray

5 eggs

½ cup oil

1 cup applesauce

1 cup crushed pineapple with juice

¾ cup sugar

½ teaspoon salt

¼ teaspoon ground cinnamon

12 ounces wide egg noodles, cooked according to the package directions

1. Preheat the oven to 350°F. Grease a 12-cup muffin tin with cooking spray.
2. In a large bowl, whisk together the eggs, oil, applesauce, crushed pineapple, sugar, salt, and cinnamon. Add the cooked noodles to the bowl and mix well.
3. Divide the batter evenly among the prepared muffin cups.
4. Bake for 20 to 25 minutes or until the muffins are set and the edges are slightly crusty.

Make-ahead Tip: This recipe freezes well. You can prep and cook the muffins in advance and store them in the freezer in an airtight container for up to 6 months.

Per serving: Calories: 278; Total fat: 12g; Total carbs: 37g; Fiber: 1g; Sugar: 17g; Protein: 6g; Sodium: 129mg

Matzo Pancakes (Brei)

P PAREVE NUT FREE **V** VEGETARIAN

SERVES 6 TO 8 | PREP TIME: 10 MINUTES | COOK TIME: 20 MINUTES

Matzo Brei is a traditional food served on Passover, when fermented grains are not allowed. It is basically a pancake made of crushed matzo and eggs. It's usually served plain or topped with a sprinkling of cinnamon and sugar. I like to add caramelized bananas and chocolate chips for some added sweetness. You can also go in a savory direction by adding chopped pastrami or corned beef with a creamy, dairy-free dressing on top.

4 matzo sheets

3 eggs

Salt

Freshly ground
black pepper

2 tablespoons canola oil

Sugar and ground
cinnamon, for serving

1. In a large bowl, break the matzo into pieces, cover with water, and soak until the matzo softens.

2. In a separate large bowl, whisk the eggs with a pinch of salt and pepper.

3. Drain the matzo, gently squeezing excess water from the mixture, and add it to the bowl with the eggs.

4. Heat the oil in a large skillet over medium-high heat. Working in batches, drop spoonfuls of the batter into the hot oil and fry until golden brown on both sides.

5. Sprinkle with sugar and cinnamon before serving.

Variation Tip: You can also top these pancakes with caramelized bananas: Thinly slice a few bananas, coat the slices in sugar, and cook them in a nonstick skillet over low heat until the sugar has caramelized and the bananas turn golden brown. You can also add chocolate chips directly to the matzo batter before frying. On the other hand, if you like things savory, you can top the pancakes with kraut, Russian dressing, and chopped corned beef for a Reuben version.

Per serving: Calories: 146; Total fat: 7g; Total carbs: 16g; Fiber: 1g; Sugar: 0g; Protein: 5g; Sodium: 58mg

Quinoa Salad with Avocado and Pomegranate Seeds

P PAREVE **G** GLUTEN FREE **⊘** NUT FREE **V** VEGAN

SERVES 6 TO 8 | PREP TIME: 10 MINUTES | COOK TIME: 20 MINUTES

Quinoa is the perfect base for a salad. It's hearty and filling and its neutral flavor works well with just about anything. Diced avocado adds a smooth texture to the dish, while pomegranate arils give it a nice pop of color and added crunch. This recipe is a holiday and Shabbat menu staple of mine, since it's tasty, simple to prepare, and—bonus—pretty to look at.

1 cup quinoa

2 cups vegetable stock

1 avocado, cubed

1 small red onion, diced

½ cup pomegranate arils

⅓ cup olive oil

1 tablespoon balsamic vinegar

½ tablespoon brown sugar

¼ teaspoon garlic powder

¼ teaspoon salt

¼ teaspoon freshly ground black pepper

Juice of 1 lime

1. Rinse the quinoa in a fine-mesh sieve until the water runs clear, then drain well and transfer the quinoa to a medium pot.

2. Add the stock to the quinoa in the pot and bring to a boil. Cover the pot with a lid, reduce the heat to low, and simmer until the stock is absorbed, 15 to 20 minutes.

3. Remove the pot from the heat and let it sit for about 4 minutes before uncovering and fluffing the quinoa with a fork.

4. Transfer the cooked quinoa to a large serving bowl and add the avocado, red onion, and pomegranate arils.

5. In a small bowl, prepare the dressing by whisking together the olive oil, balsamic vinegar, brown sugar, garlic powder, salt, pepper, and lime juice. Pour the dressing over the salad and mix well.

Per serving: Calories: 288; Total fat: 18g; Total carbs: 30g; Fiber: 5g; Sugar: 8g; Protein: 5g; Sodium: 358mg

Reuben–Stuffed Latkes

 MEAT   NUT FREE

SERVES 12 TO 15 | PREP TIME: 10 MINUTES | COOK TIME: 20 MINUTES

Hanukkah is a time for fried food—we fry classics like latkes and donuts to remember the miracle of one tiny jug of oil lasting eight whole nights. (In other words, we basically get eight nights to stuff our faces with fried food, and that's why Hanukkah is one of my favorite holidays.) A classic latke is made with shredded potatoes, onions, eggs, a bit of flour to hold it together, and some salt and pepper. Once you have the classic recipe down, you can enjoy it in *so* many different tasty ways. In this dish the latkes are stuffed with chopped corned beef and topped, Reuben–style, with kraut, Russian dressing, and more corned beef.

1 pound frozen hash browns, defrosted

1 small onion, chopped

2 eggs

2 tablespoons all-purpose flour

1 teaspoon salt

¼ teaspoon freshly ground black pepper

6 ounces corned beef, chopped, plus ¼ cup for serving

2 tablespoons canola oil, plus more as needed

½ cup Russian dressing, for serving

1 cup sauerkraut, for serving

1. In a large mixing bowl, combine the hash browns, onion, eggs, flour, salt, pepper, and 6 ounces of corned beef.

2. Heat the oil in a large skillet over medium-high heat.

3. When the oil is hot, drop mounds of the batter into the skillet, using a tablespoon for bite-size latkes and an ice cream scoop for larger latkes. Fry until both sides are golden brown and remove them to a plate. (Be careful not to flip the latkes over until the edges are slightly browned.) Before each new batch, add more oil to the skillet if needed and make sure you let it heat up again. The oil should sizzle!

4. Serve the latkes with Russian dressing, kraut, and the reserved ¼ cup of chopped corned beef.

Variation Tip: Think of the classic potato latke as a slice of bread, and top it with any of your usual sandwich toppings: tuna with spicy mayo and scallions, shredded barbecue chicken, melted cheese, marinara sauce with veggies, miniature burgers, etc. You can also add other ingredients to the potato base before frying, such as steamed broccoli and Cheddar cheese. (Please note: these suggestions contain both meat and dairy ideas and are not meant to be cooked at the same time.)

Per serving: Calories: 225; Total fat: 15g; Total carbs: 19g; Fiber: 2g; Sugar: 4g; Protein: 4g; Sodium: 537mg

Vegetable Basmati Rice with Honey

P PAREVE **⊘** NUT FREE **SF** SUGAR FREE **V** VEGETARIAN

SERVES 6 TO 8 | PREP TIME: 10 MINUTES | COOK TIME: 30 MINUTES

This is another classic, easy recipe from my big sis Tova. She is always saving the day (and my meal prep stress) with quick and tasty recipes that my kids will gobble up. This rice with a vegetable medley of onions, mushrooms, carrots, and peppers is flavorful and filling and can accompany any main dish from chicken or salmon to tofu. The finishing drizzle of honey adds the ultimate flavor boost.

1 tablespoon canola oil

1 onion, chopped

1 carrot, peeled and grated

1 red bell pepper, seeded and cut lengthwise into strips

8 ounces sliced mushrooms

2 cups basmati rice

4 cups water

1 tablespoon honey

1. Heat the oil in a large pot.
2. Add the onion, carrot, red pepper, and mushrooms. Cook until slightly browned, 5 to 7 minutes, then add the rice and water to the pot and cook, uncovered, on medium-low heat until the water is absorbed, 15 to 20 minutes.
3. Fluff the rice with a fork, drizzle with the honey, and stir well to combine.

Variation Tip: You can also make this in the oven: Place all the ingredients (including the honey) in a baking pan, cover, and bake at 350°F for about 45 minutes or until the water is absorbed and the rice is soft and fluffy. If you want to add a protein, you can top the rice with chicken pieces and bake them together with the rice for an easy one-pan meal.

Per serving: Calories: 282; Total fat: 3g; Total carbs: 58g; Fiber: 2g; Sugar: 6g; Protein: 6g; Sodium: 14mg

Gluten-Free Egg "Noodles"

P PAREVE **G** GLUTEN FREE **GF** GRAIN FREE **⊘** NUT FREE **SF** SUGAR FREE **V** VEGETARIAN

SERVES 6 TO 8 | PREP TIME: 10 MINUTES | COOK TIME: 20 MINUTES

These simple gluten-free egg "noodles" taste like a miracle on Passover. When all pasta (and gluten) is off the menu and you are craving something to slurp in your chicken soup, these will be the most wonderful thing on your plate (or bowl). You can serve them in soup or with meatballs, or you can eat them as crêpes with chocolate chips or raspberry jam on top. Serve them year-round, whenever you want a gluten-free option.

6 eggs

1 cup water

1 cup potato starch

Canola oil, for frying

1. In a large mixing bowl, combine the eggs, water, and potato starch.

2. Coat a large skillet with cooking oil and place it over medium-high heat.

3. Using a 1-cup measure, scoop some of the batter into the skillet, tilting the skillet so the batter spreads out evenly. Cook until the crêpe looks dry (you do not need to cook both sides), then flip it onto a cutting board and repeat until all the batter is used.

4. Once the crêpes are cooked, roll each one and slice it crosswise to create thin "noodles."

Per serving: Calories: 211; Total fat: 9g; Total carbs: 27g; Fiber: 0g; Sugar: 0g; Protein: 6g; Sodium: 62mg

Broccoli Cheddar Bites

① DAIRY ♥ FAMILY FAVORITE ⊘ NUT FREE Ⓥ VEGETARIAN

SERVES 15 TO 20 | PREP TIME: 10 MINUTES | COOK TIME: 30 MINUTES

When I create a menu for entertaining, I like to think ahead. No one wants to be the first to slice into a beautifully plated quiche or savory pie—but noshing on a few broccoli bites? No one will notice if you dig in early. These savory broccoli Cheddar bites are perfectly sized (and delicious) party food. Pile them up on a platter next to a few dipping sauce options (barbecue sauce and creamy dill sauce are my favorites), and watch them disappear one by one.

2 heads broccoli, chopped

2 eggs

2 cups shredded Cheddar cheese

½ cup cream cheese, at room temperature

1¼ cups breadcrumbs, divided

½ teaspoon salt

½ teaspoon freshly ground black pepper

¼ teaspoon garlic powder

¼ teaspoon cayenne pepper

Nonstick cooking spray

1. Preheat the oven to 375°F.

2. Place the chopped broccoli in a microwave-safe dish with a splash of water, and microwave for 4 to 5 minutes or until softened.

3. Transfer the broccoli to a large mixing bowl and mash it with a potato masher. Add the eggs, Cheddar, cream cheese, ¼ cup of breadcrumbs, salt, pepper, garlic powder, and cayenne pepper. Mix well until combined.

4. Wet your hands and shape the broccoli mixture into balls (about 1 tablespoon each).

5. Line a baking sheet with parchment paper. Coat the broccoli balls with the remaining breadcrumbs, then place them on the baking sheet.

6. Spray the bites with cooking spray, then bake them for 20 to 25 minutes, until slightly crispy.

Variation Tip: Stuff Cheddar cubes inside the broccoli bites for a super cheesy filling! You can also make a quiche: Place the mixture in a prepared piecrust and bake for about 45 minutes. Top the quiches with breadcrumbs and extra shredded Cheddar cheese if desired.

Per serving (1 bite): Calories: 148; Total fat: 9g; Total carbs: 10g; Fiber: 1g; Sugar: 1g; Protein: 8g; Sodium: 287mg

Barbecue Pastrami–Wrapped Asparagus

MEAT · **EASY PREP** · **GF GRAIN FREE** · **NUT FREE**

SERVES 6 TO 8 | PREP TIME: 10 MINUTES | COOK TIME: 15 MINUTES

This savory, saucy dish is the perfect appetizer for entertaining. Slightly crispy asparagus wrapped up in tender strips of pastrami, smothered in tangy barbecue sauce—it is so addictive that I will often eat several pieces myself before the meal even begins. This is a fan favorite for both adults and children, who often enjoy licking off the barbecue sauce before noshing on the pastrami and asparagus.

Nonstick cooking spray

½ pound pastrami, thinly sliced

1 cup barbecue sauce

1 bunch asparagus (about 13 stalks), tough ends snapped off and discarded

1. Preheat the oven to 400°F. Grease a baking sheet with nonstick cooking spray.

2. Brush both sides of each pastrami slice with barbecue sauce, then wrap them around the asparagus spears.

3. Place the wrapped asparagus on the prepared baking sheet, brush them with the remaining barbecue sauce, and bake for 10 to 12 minutes.

Per serving: Calories: 126; Total fat: 2g; Total carbs: 17g; Fiber: 1g; Sugar: 11g; Protein: 9g; Sodium: 802mg

Perfectly Creamy Mac and Cheese

DAIRY ● **FAMILY FAVORITE** ● **NUT FREE** **SF** **SUGAR FREE** **V** **VEGETARIAN**

SERVES 6 TO 8 | PREP TIME: 12 MINUTES | COOK TIME: 10 MINUTES

I love a good, thick sauce over pasta, and this easy mac and cheese recipe is a classic that both adults and children will enjoy. If you want to make it a touch healthier, add steamed broccoli or cauliflower to the sauce once it has thickened. Leftovers (if you have any) can be baked in egg roll wrappers to make crispy treats. This Cheddar sauce is also delicious served over baked potatoes or tortilla chips with guacamole and salsa.

2 tablespoons butter

2 tablespoons all-purpose flour

2 cups whole milk

1 teaspoon mustard powder

Salt

Freshly ground black pepper

1 cup shredded Cheddar cheese

1 cup shredded mozzarella cheese

1 (1-pound) box medium shell pasta, cooked and drained

1. In a large pot over medium heat, melt the butter. When the butter is bubbly, add the flour and whisk until a paste forms. Slowly add the milk in a gentle stream, whisking until it is fully incorporated without any lumps of flour. Cook over medium-high heat, stirring constantly, until the sauce has thickened.

2. Remove the pot from the heat and add the mustard powder, salt and pepper to taste, and the Cheddar and mozzarella cheeses. Stir until the cheese is melted and the sauce is smooth.

3. Add the cooked pasta to the pot and mix well before serving.

Variation Tip: To create a crunchy topping, place the mac and cheese in a large greased baking dish and top with ½ cup panko breadcrumbs and ½ cup grated Parmesan cheese. Bake at 350°F for 15 to 20 minutes, until the crust is crispy and the cheese is bubbling. You can also bake it with the topping in individual ramekins.

Per serving: Calories: 494; Total fat: 18g; Total carbs: 64g; Fiber: 3g; Sugar: 6g; Protein: 22g; Sodium: 324mg

Teriyaki Grilled Tofu

P PAREVE GF GRAIN FREE NUT FREE V VEGETARIAN

SERVES 4 TO 5 | PREP TIME: 10 MINUTES | COOK TIME: 12 MINUTES

Going meatless doesn't have to mean skimping on flavor. The glaze in this recipe is good enough to eat solo, but it tastes even better drizzled over vegetables and grilled tofu. If it gets on everything else on your plate in the process, all the better. Make sure to press the tofu (see Ingredient Tip) to extract all the moisture and get perfectly cooked tofu every time.

2 tablespoons canola oil

1 (12-ounce) package extra-firm tofu, patted dry and pressed to remove moisture (see Ingredient Tip), then cut into triangles

4 tablespoons soy sauce

2 tablespoons rice vinegar

¼ cup honey

2 garlic cloves, minced

1 teaspoon peeled and minced fresh ginger

4 cups steamed green beans, for serving

1. Heat the oil in a grill pan over medium heat. When the pan is hot, add the tofu triangles and grill them for 2 to 3 minutes per side or until grill marks appear.

2. Meanwhile, in a medium saucepan over medium-high heat, combine the soy sauce, rice vinegar, honey, garlic, and ginger and stir until the mixture thickens.

3. Serve the tofu over the steamed green beans, and drizzle the glaze over the top.

Ingredient Tip: Tofu should always be pressed before baking or grilling. Tofu contains a large amount of moisture, which can cause it to fall apart when cooking; the pressing process helps it maintain its shape. Place a layer of folded paper towels on a cutting board, set the tofu on top, and place another layer of folded paper towels on top of the tofu. Place a weighted item such as another cutting board or a bowl on top of the tofu, and lightly push down on it. The idea is to squeeze out as much moisture as possible. When cooking a dish with tofu, I like to set this on the counter before I even begin the cooking process. Then, when I am ready to start on dinner, the tofu is ready to slice and grill.

Per serving: Calories: 268; Total fat: 13g; Total carbs: 29g; Fiber: 4g; Sugar: 20g; Protein: 13g; Sodium: 918mg

Crispy Tofu Wraps with Avocado and Barbecue Sauce

 PAREVE  NUT FREE **V** VEGETARIAN

SERVES 4 TO 5 | PREP TIME: 10 MINUTES | COOK TIME: 20 MINUTES

I wasn't a huge fan of tofu until I tried it coated in cornflake crumbs, baked until crispy, and dipped in sauce. One bite and I was hooked. It's basically a meat-free schnitzel, and it can be served any way you would normally serve crispy chicken: dipped in sweet chili sauce; in a salad with creamy dill sauce; or, as here, in a lettuce wrap with tomatoes, avocado, and onion smothered with creamy barbecue sauce.

FOR THE CREAMY BARBECUE SAUCE

½ cup ketchup

½ cup mayonnaise

½ cup barbecue sauce

FOR THE WRAPS

Nonstick cooking spray

2 eggs

¼ teaspoon freshly ground black pepper

½ teaspoon salt

¼ teaspoon garlic powder

¼ teaspoon paprika

1 cup cornflake crumbs

1 (12-ounce) package extra-firm tofu, pressed (see page 43) and cut into thin rectangles

4 or 5 large tortillas

Romaine lettuce or spinach

1 tomato, sliced

1 avocado, sliced

TO MAKE THE CREAMY BARBECUE SAUCE

In a medium bowl, mix together the ketchup, mayonnaise, and barbecue sauce until creamy.

TO MAKE THE WRAPS

1. Preheat the oven to 400°F. Grease a baking sheet with cooking spray.

2. Whisk the eggs together in a large mixing bowl and season with the pepper, salt, garlic powder, and paprika.

3. Place the cornflake crumbs in a large, shallow dish.

4. Coat the tofu in the egg, then dip it into the cornflake crumbs, turning to coat the pieces evenly.

5. Place the coated tofu on the prepared baking sheet and bake for about 20 minutes, until the edges are slightly crispy.

6. Serve the tofu wrapped in the tortillas, along with the lettuce, tomato, avocado, and creamy barbecue sauce.

Variation Tip: Cut the tofu into smaller pieces before breading and baking, and serve them over a salad as croutons. You can also turn them into tofu fries by cutting them into sticks before breading them; serve them with any of your favorite dipping sauces, such as sweet chili or sweet and sour sauce or—my personal favorite—Creamy Dill Sauce (page 137).

Per serving: Calories: 600; Total fat: 27g; Total carbs: 78g; Fiber: 8g; Sugar: 21g; Protein: 18g; Sodium: 1585mg

Falafel Tacos

 PAREVE　 NUT FREE　**SF** SUGAR FREE　**V** VEGAN

SERVES 6 TO 8 | PREP TIME: 10 MINUTES | COOK TIME: 20 MINUTES

I love all kinds of Israeli food, like shawarma, sabich, and shakshuka, but the taste and texture of falafel make it my favorite. With this dish, I finally merged my love of falafel and tacos into one delicious handheld meal. Crispy falafel balls served in soft tortillas with creamy hummus, tahini, and za'atar is a match made in foodie heaven.

FOR THE FALAFEL BALLS

2½ cups canned chickpeas (garbanzo beans), rinsed and drained

1 small bunch flat-leaf parsley (about 1 cup chopped)

1 small bunch cilantro (about 1 cup chopped)

½ teaspoon salt

¼ teaspoon chili powder or cayenne pepper

2 teaspoons ground cumin

2 tablespoons all-purpose flour

2 tablespoons canola oil, for frying

FOR THE TACOS

6 tablespoons Classic Hummus (page 14)

6 small to medium soft tortillas or hard taco shells

1 cup shredded purple cabbage

⅓ cup tahini

Za'atar spice blend

Hot sauce for serving (optional)

TO MAKE THE FALAFEL BALLS

1. In a food processor, process the chickpeas, parsley, cilantro, salt, chili powder, cumin, and flour until a paste forms. (It's okay if it's slightly chunky, as that will just add to the texture of the falafel.) The flour is what binds the ingredients, so if the balls fall apart when frying, add more flour to the batter.

2. In a large skillet, heat the oil.

3. Using an ice cream scoop, scoop balls of the falafel mixture into the oil and fry until both sides are lightly browned, about 5 minutes per side. Use the back of the scoop to gently flatten the ball after flipping, as this will create more of a burger shape.

TO MAKE THE TACOS

1. Spread the hummus over the tortillas and top with the shredded cabbage and falafel balls.

2. Drizzle the tahini on top and season with za'atar. You can also crumble up extra falafel balls to garnish the tacos, and add a splash of hot sauce (if using) for a nice spicy kick.

Variation Tip: Stuff falafel balls with cubed mozzarella, Cheddar, or goat cheese for a delicious filling. Serve falafel over Israeli salad (diced cucumbers, tomatoes, and red onion, seasoned with olive oil, salt, pepper, and fresh lemon juice) with tahini drizzled on top, or as sliders in buns.

Per serving: Calories: 395; Total fat: 17g; Total carbs: 51g; Fiber: 9g; Sugar: 5g; Protein: 14g; Sodium: 673mg

Kani Bites with Creamy Dill Sauce

P PAREVE NUT FREE **SF** SUGAR FREE

MAKES 20 BITES | **PREP TIME: 15 MINUTES** | **COOK TIME: 15 MINUTES**

These mock crab (kani) balls are fantastic—and they're an excellent party food, since you can prepare them up to a day in advance and serve them at room temperature. I usually make a double batch, since they are such a crowd pleaser and a personal favorite of mine. Serve them lined up on a platter over fresh parsley leaves with creamy dill sauce. Or go rustic and coat them in cornflake crumbs before baking, then serve as sliders in buns!

2 eggs

½ cup mayonnaise

¼ cup chopped celery

2 tablespoons chopped fresh parsley

2 teaspoons Dijon mustard

½ teaspoon salt

½ teaspoon Montreal steak seasoning

½ cup breadcrumbs

6 kani sticks, diced

Creamy Dill Sauce (page 137), for serving

1. Preheat the oven to 400°F.

2. In a large mixing bowl, combine the eggs, mayonnaise, celery, parsley, mustard, salt, Montreal steak seasoning, breadcrumbs, and kani.

3. Lightly grease a baking sheet. Shape the mixture into balls about the size of 1 tablespoon, and place them on the baking sheet. Bake for 15 minutes or until firm and slightly crispy at the edges.

4. Serve with creamy dill sauce for dipping.

Per serving (1 bite): Calories: 47; Total fat: 3g; Total carbs: 5g; Fiber: 1g; Sugar: 1g; Protein: 1g; Sodium: 174mg

Salmon with Lemon Caper Sauce

P PAREVE GF GRAIN FREE NUT FREE SF SUGAR FREE

SERVES 4 TO 5 | PREP TIME: 10 MINUTES | COOK TIME: 20 MINUTES

I really enjoy the taste and presentation of the lemon caper sauce layered over the fish in this dish, and I often serve it when entertaining. Guests usually end up asking for more of the delicious sauce, so I make sure to provide a serving dish of it on the table for easy access.

2 pounds salmon fillets

1 tablespoon olive oil

Juice of 1 lemon, divided

1½ teaspoons salt, divided

¼ teaspoon plus ⅛ teaspoon freshly ground black pepper

2 tablespoons Earth Balance

1 tablespoon all-purpose flour

1 cup water (or vegetable stock or white wine)

2 tablespoons capers

1. Preheat the oven to 400°F.

2. Line a baking dish with parchment paper. Place the salmon in the baking dish and drizzle with the olive oil and half the lemon juice. Season with 1 teaspoon of salt and ¼ teaspoon of pepper.

3. Bake for about 18 minutes, until the salmon flakes easily with a fork.

4. While the salmon bakes, prepare the sauce: In a small saucepan, melt the Earth Balance, then add the flour and whisk until a paste forms. Add the water and stir. Season with the remaining ½ teaspoon of salt and ⅛ teaspoon of pepper and the remaining lemon juice. Whisk together until the sauce thickens, then stir in the capers.

5. Serve the salmon topped with the sauce.

Per serving: Calories: 441; Total fat: 30g; Total carbs: 2g; Fiber: 0g; Sugar: 0g; Protein: 41g; Sodium: 1011mg

Fish Tacos

 PAREVE   NUT FREE   **SF** SUGAR FREE

SERVES 4 TO 5 | PREP TIME: 15 MINUTES | COOK TIME: 15 MINUTES

My love for tacos is real, and so is my need for easy recipes that don't keep me in the kitchen for a long time—I would much rather be sitting at the dinner table enjoying the food. The zesty marinade for the tilapia creates a delicious savory taco filling of flaked fish, and the cabbage adds a nice contrasting crunch to the tomatoes. Topped with a creamy dressing of either dill sauce or cilantro-lime sauce, it's a recipe you will want in your weekly dinner rotation.

¼ cup olive oil

Juice of 1 lime

1 small red onion, diced

1 small bunch cilantro, chopped

½ teaspoon ground cumin

½ teaspoon salt

¼ teaspoon freshly ground black pepper

2 pounds tilapia fillets

4 large corn tortillas, for serving

2 tomatoes, diced, for serving

1 cup shredded cabbage, for serving

½ cup *Creamy Dill Sauce (page 137)* or *Cilantro-Lime Sauce (page 134),* for serving

1. Preheat the oven to 400°F. Line a baking sheet with parchment paper.

2. Combine the olive oil, lime juice, red onion, cilantro, cumin, salt, and pepper in a large zip-top plastic bag. Add the tilapia, seal the bag, and let it marinate for 15 minutes.

3. Place the fish on the baking sheet and bake for about 15 minutes or until the fish flakes easily with a fork. Remove the fish from the oven and, using two forks, flake it into small pieces.

4. Serve the flaked fish in the corn tortillas with the diced tomatoes, shredded cabbage, and the sauce of your choice.

Per serving: Calories: 550; Total fat: 35g; Total carbs: 16g; Fiber: 3g; Sugar: 2g; Protein: 44g; Sodium: 631mg

Creamy Pesto Tortellini with Artichokes

P PAREVE NUT FREE SF SUGAR FREE V VEGETARIAN

SERVES 5 TO 6 | PREP TIME: 15 MINUTES | COOK TIME: 15 MINUTES

This thick and creamy pesto sauce is dairy free and delicious. I love the addition of chunks of artichokes and stuffed tortellini pasta; however, you can swap them out for any variety of vegetable and shape of pasta you prefer. If you opt to keep the sauce and pasta nondairy, you can add in slices of grilled spiced chicken or shredded rotisserie chicken for an even more filling dish.

1 (12-ounce) package dairy-free tortellini pasta

2 tablespoons Earth Balance

2 tablespoons all-purpose flour

2 cups soy milk

2 tablespoons store-bought dairy-free pesto sauce

½ teaspoon salt

½ teaspoon freshly ground black pepper

½ teaspoon garlic powder

1 (12-ounce) can artichoke hearts, drained

Chopped fresh basil, for serving (optional)

Red pepper flakes, for serving (optional)

1. Cook the pasta in salted boiling water until al dente; drain and set it aside.

2. In a large pot over medium heat, melt the Earth Balance. Add the flour and whisk together until smooth and combined. Add the milk and whisk together until smooth and combined. When the mixture begins to thicken, stir in the pesto, salt, pepper, garlic powder, and artichoke hearts. Once the sauce is nice and thick, turn off the heat and fold in the pasta.

3. Mix well and serve with freshly chopped basil and red pepper flakes (if using).

Variation Tip: If you don't like artichokes, you can leave them out completely or replace them with wilted spinach or sautéed mushrooms and onions. If you want to make this dairy, simply use butter instead of Earth Balance and use cow's milk or heavy cream instead of soy milk. If you do not make the sauce dairy, you can add slices of cooked chicken to the sauce.

Per serving: Calories: 378; Total fat: 14g; Total carbs: 49g; Fiber: 5g; Sugar: 6g; Protein: 14g; Sodium: 615mg

CLASSIC POTATO KUGEL *page 59*

Chapter Four

5 INGREDIENTS

Sausage Egg Muffins

MEAT · **EASY PREP** · **G** GLUTEN FREE · **GF** GRAIN FREE · **NUT FREE** · **SF** SUGAR FREE

MAKES 12 MUFFINS | PREP TIME: 15 MINUTES | COOK TIME: 25 MINUTES

I like my breakfast foods both sweet and savory. When I'm not making pancakes and waffles, I am usually eating breakfast tacos stuffed with scrambled eggs, salsa, and avocado—or these filling muffins loaded with onion, pepper, mushrooms, and sausage. You can easily make an extra batch of this recipe and have the muffins ready to go when you want a quick bite in the morning.

1 tablespoon olive oil, plus more for greasing

1 large yellow onion, diced

8 ounces mushrooms, sliced

1 large red bell pepper, diced

4 kosher sausage links, diced

12 eggs

Salt

Freshly ground black pepper

1. Preheat the oven to 350°F. Grease a 12-cup muffin pan with olive oil.

2. In a large skillet over medium-high heat, heat the olive oil. Add the onion, mushrooms, and red pepper, cook until slightly browned, then add the diced sausage and cook until the sausage is browned at the edges.

3. Scoop 1 to 2 tablespoons of the sausage mixture into each cup in the muffin pan and spread evenly.

4. Separate the yolks and whites of 6 of the eggs. Whisk the remaining 6 eggs with the 6 egg whites. Season with salt and pepper. (Discard the extra yolks or reserve them for another use.)

5. Pour the egg mixture over the veggie-sausage mixture in the muffin pan, distributing evenly, and bake for 20 to 25 minutes, until the eggs are set.

Make-ahead Tip: These muffins can be prepared in advance and frozen in an airtight container. Simply reheat in the oven or microwave when it is time to eat.

Per serving (1 muffin): Calories: 127; Total fat: 8g; Total carbs: 4g; Fiber: 1g; Sugar: 2g; Protein: 11g; Sodium: 235mg

Barbecue Cauliflower Poppers

(P) PAREVE   **(*) EASY PREP**   **(♥) FAMILY FAVORITE**   **(V) VEGETARIAN**

SERVES 6 TO 8 | PREP TIME: 10 MINUTES | COOK TIME: 25 MINUTES

I'm the girl who shows up to the game day party with snacks. Lots of them. I don't know much about sports (sorry, Pops!), but I do know what to serve while you are watching them, and these barbecue poppers are on the list. With a crispy coating layered around tasty barbecue sauce and melt-in-your-mouth cauliflower, this dish makes for perfect finger-licking game food. It's also a great recipe to have on hand when you want an easy meatless meal.

¼ cup barbecue sauce

¼ cup mayonnaise

1 cup cornflake crumbs (or breadcrumbs)

1 head cauliflower, cut into bite-size florets

1. Preheat the oven to 450°F. Line a baking sheet with parchment paper.
2. In a small bowl, mix together the barbecue sauce and mayonnaise.
3. Place the cornflake crumbs in a shallow dish.
4. Dip the cauliflower pieces into the barbecue sauce mixture, then roll them in the cornflake crumbs.
5. Place the coated cauliflower on the prepared baking sheet and bake for 20 to 25 minutes, until they are crispy on the outside. (I like a crunchy coating with slightly burnt edges.)

Ingredient Tip: To save time in the kitchen, you can use frozen cauliflower pieces.

Per serving: Calories: 117; Total fat: 7g; Total carbs: 13g; Fiber: 6g; Sugar: 6g; Protein: 2g; Sodium: 241mg

Sausage-Stuffed Sweet Potatoes

 MEAT EASY PREP **GF** GRAIN FREE NUT FREE **SF** SUGAR FREE

SERVES 5 | PREP TIME: 10 MINUTES | COOK TIME: 15 MINUTES

This is one of my favorite meals to cook, serve, and eat, since it's super easy to prep, looks fabulous on a plate, and tastes amazing. It's great on a busy school night and pretty enough for Shabbat dinner or the holidays.

5 medium sweet
potatoes

1 tablespoon olive oil

1 large onion, thinly sliced

1 large bell pepper
(any color), cut into
thin strips

4 sausage links (12-ounce
package of any flavor
sausage), cut into
thin rounds

5 teaspoons Earth
Balance (optional)

Dijon mustard,
for serving

Chopped fresh cilantro,
for serving (optional)

Per serving: Calories: 377;
Total fat: 23g; Total carbs: 32g;
Fiber: 6g; Sugar: 8g; Protein: 11g;
Sodium: 821mg

1. Preheat the oven to 350°F. Line a baking sheet with parchment paper.

2. Pierce the potatoes on all sides with a fork, then place them on the prepared baking sheet. Bake for about 1 hour, until soft. Remove from the oven and set aside to cool slightly.

3. In a large skillet over medium heat, heat the oil. Add the onion, pepper, and sausages, and cook until nicely browned, stirring every so often.

4. Once the potatoes have cooled a bit, slice them down the middle but not all the way through. You want to create a pocket to fill up with the sausage mixture. Mash the insides of the potatoes with a fork, adding the Earth Balance (if using).

5. Fill the potatoes with the sausage-pepper mixture. Drizzle with Dijon mustard and garnish with cilantro (if using).

Variation Tip: There are tons of ways to mix up this recipe: Swap the sausage for hot dogs, sub in chopped chives or parsley for the cilantro, or try a different veggie combo (mushrooms and zucchini are delicious). Instead of mustard, you can serve these topped with barbecue sauce, hot sauce, Cilantro-Lime Sauce (page 134), or sweet chili sauce.

Oven-Roasted Tomato Soup

P PAREVE **G** GLUTEN FREE **GF** GRAIN FREE **◇** NUT FREE **SF** SUGAR FREE **V** VEGAN

SERVES 4 TO 5 | PREP TIME: 15 MINUTES | COOK TIME: 1 HOUR 10 MINUTES

This dinner is tasty and fun for both adults and children. Grown-ups will enjoy the rich flavor of the roasted tomatoes in the soup, while children will adore the mini grilled cheese sandwiches skewered on top (see Variation Tip).

1 pint cherry tomatoes

2 tablespoons olive oil, divided

Salt

Freshly ground black pepper

1 small yellow onion, diced

2 garlic cloves, chopped

1 (14.5-ounce) can diced fire-roasted tomatoes

3 cups vegetable stock

1. Preheat the oven to 400°F. Line a baking sheet with parchment paper.

2. Place the cherry tomatoes on the prepared baking sheet and drizzle them with 1 tablespoon of olive oil; season with salt and pepper to taste and toss well to coat. Roast the tomatoes for 30 to 35 minutes, until they blister and begin to brown.

3. In a large pot, heat the remaining 1 tablespoon of oil and sauté the onion and garlic until the onion is translucent. Add the roasted tomatoes and cook for 2 minutes, then add the canned tomatoes and cook for another 2 to 5 minutes. Stir in the stock and bring the mixture to a boil, then reduce the heat to low and simmer for 30 minutes.

4. Using an immersion blender, purée the soup before serving.

Variation Tip: This soup is delicious served with grilled cheese sandwiches cut into bite-size pieces. I skewer together the pieces and serve them over the soup as croutons.

Make-ahead Tip: You can roast the tomatoes in advance; store them in an airtight container in the refrigerator until you are ready to make the soup.

Per serving: Calories: 108; Total fat: 7g; Total carbs: 9g; Fiber: 2g; Sugar: 5g; Protein: 5g; Sodium: 703mg

Spinach Quinoa Patties

(P) PAREVE (G) GLUTEN FREE (⌒) NUT FREE (SF) SUGAR FREE (V) VEGETARIAN

MAKES 12 TO 15 PATTIES | PREP TIME: 10 MINUTES | COOK TIME: 15 MINUTES

These patties are packed with not just one but two superfoods, spinach and quinoa, which means double the nutrients and flavor. They can be served solo or topped with western sauce (equal parts barbecue sauce, ketchup, and mayonnaise) and tomatoes, onions, and lettuce for a filling meatless burger. Or, if you desire a dairy option, stuff the center of the patties with cubes of Cheddar, feta, or goat cheese for a savory surprise.

3 tablespoons olive oil, divided

1 small yellow onion, diced

1 (8-ounce) package frozen spinach (thawed)

2½ cups cooked quinoa

1 teaspoon salt

⅛ teaspoon freshly ground black pepper

½ teaspoon garlic powder

⅛ teaspoon cayenne pepper (optional)

2 eggs

1. In a large skillet over medium-high heat, heat 1 tablespoon of oil, add the onion and spinach, and cook until the onion is tender.

2. Scrape the onion-spinach mixture into a large bowl and add the quinoa. Season with the salt, pepper, garlic powder, and cayenne pepper (if using), then add the eggs and mix well.

3. In the skillet over medium-high heat, heat the remaining 2 tablespoons of olive oil. Using a tablespoon measure for small patties or an ice cream scoop for larger ones, scoop patties onto the skillet and cook until golden brown on both sides.

Variation Tip: You can also bake the patties in a 350°F oven for 15 to 18 minutes. Be sure to grease the baking pan so they don't stick.

Per serving: Calories: 178; Total fat: 7g; Total carbs: 24g; Fiber: 3g; Sugar: 0g; Protein: 7g; Sodium: 221mg

Classic Potato Kugel

P PAREVE **G** GLUTEN FREE **GF** GRAIN FREE **◇** NUT FREE **SF** SUGAR FREE **V** VEGETARIAN

SERVES 8 TO 10 | PREP TIME: 15 MINUTES | COOK TIME: 45 MINUTES

My mom's potato kugel is perfection. With a creamy center, crispy edges, and a golden crust, it's the ultimate Jewish comfort food. I have memories of hanging around the kitchen on Thursday nights watching as my mother would prepare food for Shabbat. This recipe is a classic for Passover.

6 medium russet potatoes, peeled and cut into large chunks

1 onion, peeled and quartered

3 eggs

¾ cup canola oil

1 teaspoon salt

¼ teaspoon freshly ground black pepper

1. Preheat the oven to 350°F. Line a 9-by-13-inch baking dish with parchment paper.

2. In a food processor, shred the potatoes and onion.

3. In a large mixing bowl, combine the shredded potatoes and onion with the eggs, oil, salt, and pepper. Scrape the mixture into the prepared baking dish.

4. Bake for 30 to 45 minutes, until the top is golden and the edges are crispy.

Per serving: Calories: 320; Total fat: 22g; Total carbs: 27g; Fiber: 4g; Sugar: 3g; Protein: 5g; Sodium: 324mg

Lazy Meatballs

 MEAT FAMILY FAVORITE NUT FREE **SF** SUGAR FREE

SERVES 4 TO 5 | PREP TIME: 15 MINUTES | COOK TIME: 1 HOUR

People don't often believe me when I say I'm lazy in the kitchen, since cooking is my job—but I'm just here for the food. And in this case, I'm here for the meatballs. This dish, with only a few ingredients and minimal prep, is a menu must and a family favorite. If you want a grain-free version, swap out the breadcrumbs for almond meal or coconut flour.

1 (24-ounce) jar marinara sauce

1 cup water

1 pound ground beef

2 eggs

½ cup breadcrumbs

Chopped fresh parsley or dried Italian herbs, for serving

1. In a large pot over high heat, combine the marinara sauce and water. Bring to a boil, then reduce the heat to low.

2. In a large mixing bowl, combine the ground beef, eggs, and breadcrumbs. (Don't overmix! That creates a tough meatball.) Form the beef mixture into balls using a tablespoon measure.

3. Place the meatballs in the simmering sauce and cook for about 1 hour or until they are cooked through.

4. Serve sprinkled with chopped fresh parsley or dried Italian herbs.

Variation Tip: Swap the water for 1 cup coconut milk to yield a creamier, coconut-infused sauce. If you want a creamy sauce without the coconut flavor, you can use almond milk or soy milk.

Per serving: Calories: 277; Total fat: 11g; Total carbs: 17g; Fiber: 3g; Sugar: 8g; Protein: 29g; Sodium: 987mg

Chicken Meatballs with Celery and Carrots

MEAT ♥ FAMILY FAVORITE ⒼGLUTEN FREE ⒼⒻGRAIN FREE ⊘NUT FREE ⓈⒻSUGAR FREE

SERVES 4 TO 6 (MAKES ABOUT 28 MEATBALLS) | PREP TIME: 10 MINUTES | COOK TIME: 30 MINUTES

Bite-size chicken meatballs loaded with celery and carrots make a satisfying weeknight dinner that is both quick and tasty. You can serve the meatballs solo (they are really great to snack on!) or skewered together with a dipping sauce. (Sweet chili sauce is delicious.) My kids enjoy eating these meatballs stuffed in pitas with a hearty topping of ketchup.

1 pound ground chicken thighs

2 carrots, peeled and shredded

2 celery stalks, diced

1 egg

2 tablespoons finely chopped fresh parsley

1. Preheat the oven to 350°F. Line a baking sheet with parchment paper.

2. In a large bowl, mix together the ground chicken, carrots, celery, egg, and parsley, and shape the mixture into golf ball-size balls.

3. Place the meatballs on the prepared baking sheet and bake for about 20 to 30 minutes or until cooked through.

Per serving: Calories: 190; Total fat: 10g; Total carbs: 4g; Fiber: 1g; Sugar: 2g; Protein: 21g; Sodium: 111mg

Crispy Salmon Sticks

P PAREVE   ✳ EASY PREP   ♥ FAMILY FAVORITE   ◇ NUT FREE

SERVES 4 TO 5 | PREP TIME: 10 MINUTES | COOK TIME: 20 MINUTES

My children love dipping these salmon sticks in ketchup, and I enjoy the fact that this recipe makes great leftovers. If I can get two meals out of one for my time in the kitchen, I'm a happy mama! The salmon sticks are perfect for lunch served in a wrap with avocado, tomato, and any sauce you like.

1 cup mayonnaise

1 teaspoon yellow mustard

2 cups cornflake crumbs

½ teaspoon salt

¼ teaspoon freshly ground black pepper

1 pound salmon, cut into strips

1. Preheat the oven to 400°F. Line a baking sheet with parchment paper.

2. In a small bowl, mix together the mayonnaise and yellow mustard. Mix together the cornflake crumbs and the salt and pepper on a plate.

3. Dip the salmon strips in the mayonnaise-mustard mixture, then roll them in the cornflake crumbs.

4. Place the coated salmon strips on the prepared baking sheet and bake for 15 to 18 minutes or until the fish is cooked through.

Variation Tip: Swap out the salmon for boneless, skinless chicken breast, and you will have the most perfect chicken tenders: crunchy on the outside, juicy on the inside.

Per serving: Calories: 577; Total fat: 42g; Total carbs: 31g; Fiber: 1g; Sugar: 3g; Protein: 20g; Sodium: 840mg

Chicken Taco Bowls

◉ MEAT ♥ FAMILY FAVORITE ⬡ NUT FREE 🆂🅵 SUGAR FREE

SERVES 4 TO 5 | PREP TIME: 5 MINUTES | COOK TIME: 15 MINUTES

If I had to choose just one type of food to eat, it would most definitely be taco bowls: tasty protein, multiple sides, and salsa all layered under a delicious sauce—what's not to love? These chicken tacos are really simple to prepare and can be served in a bowl with rice, Mango Corn Salad (page 18), and Cilantro-Lime Sauce (page 134). You can also wrap the seasoned chicken in burritos or serve it in taco shells. My kids even love it mixed with corkscrew pasta.

1 tablespoon canola oil

1 yellow onion, thinly sliced

1 pound boneless, skinless chicken breast, cut into 1-inch pieces

1 (1.25-ounce) packet taco seasoning mix

¾ cup water

1. Heat the oil in a large skillet over medium-high heat. Add the onion and cook until translucent, then add the chicken pieces and cook until they are no longer pink.

2. Stir in the taco seasoning and water, reduce the heat to low, and simmer until the sauce has slightly thickened.

Per serving: Calories: 190; Total fat: 5g; Total carbs: 8g; Fiber: 1g; Sugar: 1g; Protein: 26g; Sodium: 585mg

Tofu Mushroom Stir-Fry

P PAREVE **GF** GRAIN FREE **⊗** NUT FREE **V** VEGETARIAN

SERVES 4 TO 5 | PREP TIME: 10 MINUTES | COOK TIME: 15 MINUTES

This easy stir-fry is ready in minutes and will make you want to lick your plate clean. The sauce is a great recipe that comes together quickly and tastes delicious with just about any type of stir-fry. You can swap mushrooms for green beans, asparagus, broccoli, peppers, or another favorite vegetable. To make it a meat recipe, you can also use chicken or steak slices in place of the tofu.

¼ cup soy sauce

¼ cup honey

1 tablespoon cornstarch

¼ cup water

1 tablespoon olive oil or avocado oil

8 ounces sliced mushrooms

1 (12-ounce) package extra-firm tofu, drained, pressed, and cubed

1. In a small bowl, whisk together the soy sauce and honey.

2. In another small bowl, whisk together the cornstarch and water.

3. Heat the oil in a large skillet over medium-high heat. Add the mushrooms and cook until they are soft and browned. Add the cubed tofu and let it heat up, then pour in the soy sauce–honey mixture.

4. Move the mushrooms and tofu to the sides of the skillet, creating an open space in the center of the skillet. Pour the cornstarch mixture into the open space and swirl the skillet over medium heat until the sauce thickens.

5. Once the sauce has thickened, combine everything together in the skillet and serve.

Per serving: Calories: 200; Total fat: 9g; Total carbs: 24g; Fiber: 1g; Sugar: 19g; Protein: 11g; Sodium: 910mg

Coconut-Crusted Tilapia

P PAREVE   **G** GLUTEN FREE   **GF** GRAIN FREE   **SF** SUGAR FREE

SERVES 4 | PREP TIME: 10 MINUTES | COOK TIME: 15 MINUTES

If you want a grain-free crust for fish or poultry, look no further than this coconut-almond combo. Once cooked, you can serve the tilapia in grain-free taco shells topped with Cilantro-Lime Sauce (page 134) or Creamy Dill Sauce (page 137).

3 eggs

1 cup almond meal

1 cup coconut powder

2 pounds tilapia fillets

2 tablespoons avocado or coconut oil

1. In a shallow bowl, whisk the eggs. Place the almond meal and coconut powder on separate plates.

2. Dredge each tilapia fillet in almond meal, dip it into the eggs (allowing excess egg to drip off), and then press it into the coconut powder on both sides.

3. In a large skillet over medium-high heat, heat the oil. Add the tilapia and cook until both sides are crispy and the fish flakes easily with a fork, about 4 minutes per side.

Variation Tip: To bake the tilapia, preheat the oven to 400°F. Place the coated tilapia on a parchment-lined baking sheet and bake for 20 to 22 minutes or until it flakes easily with a fork.

Per serving: Calories: 533; Total fat: 24g; Total carbs: 26g; Fiber: 15g; Sugar: 0g; Protein: 55g; Sodium: 133mg

Fried Gefilte Fish Patties

P PAREVE **♥** FAMILY FAVORITE **⊘** NUT FREE

SERVES 4 TO 5 | PREP TIME: 15 MINUTES | COOK TIME: 1 HOUR

I have had many, many guests say they don't like gefilte fish—until they taste this recipe, courtesy of my friend Henny, whom I've known since I was three years old. We grew up in Brooklyn as next-door neighbors, talking through our windows late into the night and walking to school together in the mornings. Most of my childhood memories include her and our love for food. She would join family dinners as an honorary member of the Baitz bunch, and I would sneak her all of the tomatoes from my salad (she was obsessed!). She gave me this recipe for fried gefilte fish patties, and it has quickly become a family favorite. Traditional gefilte fish is prepared by boiling it in a large pot of water with onions and carrots, then draining the pot and serving the fish sliced up with pieces of carrots on top. While I do enjoy the classic, I much prefer this no-fuss, deliciously fried version.

1 frozen gefilte fish loaf, thawed

1 tablespoon olive oil, plus more as needed

1 yellow onion, thinly sliced

1. Slice the gefilte fish loaf into thin patties.

2. In a large skillet, heat the olive oil and cook the onion until slightly browned. Add the fish patties and cook until lightly browned on both sides.

3. Serve the patties together with the onion slices.

Per serving: Calories: 191; Total fat: 14g; Total carbs: 3g; Fiber: 1g; Sugar: 1g; Protein: 13g; Sodium: 700mg

Spiced Salmon with Avocado Salsa

P PAREVE G GLUTEN FREE GF GRAIN FREE NUT FREE SF SUGAR FREE

SERVES 4 TO 5 | PREP TIME: 10 MINUTES | COOK TIME: 15 MINUTES

Salmon is the ultimate weeknight dinner: it's quick to cook, goes wonderfully with a variety of flavors and seasonings, and also happens to be major brain food. When roasting salmon, I like to stick to one basic recipe: drizzle olive oil on top, add spices, and cook in the oven on a high temperature for a short amount of time. The no-fuss preparation makes it an easy addition to my weekly meal plan, and alternating the toppings—creamy cilantro-lime sauce, dill sauce, peach salsa or, as here, fresh avocado salsa—keeps the dish fresh and exciting.

1 pound salmon

2 tablespoons olive oil

Salt

Freshly ground
black pepper

2 avocados, peeled
and diced

2 tablespoons chopped
fresh cilantro

1 small red onion, diced

Juice of 2 limes

1. Preheat the oven to 450°F. Line a baking sheet with parchment paper.

2. Place the salmon, skin-side down, on the prepared baking sheet. Drizzle it with the olive oil and season with salt and pepper to taste. Bake for about 12 minutes, until the fish is cooked through and flakes easily.

3. Meanwhile, prepare the avocado salsa. In a medium bowl, combine the avocados, cilantro, red onion, and lime juice.

4. Serve the salsa with the cooked salmon.

Per serving: Calories: 417; Total fat: 32g; Total carbs: 11g; Fiber: 6g; Sugar: 1g; Protein: 24g; Sodium: 112mg

Oven-Fried Chicken

 MEAT   ♥ FAMILY FAVORITE   ◯ NUT FREE

SERVES 6 TO 8 | PREP TIME: 10 MINUTES | COOK TIME: 1 HOUR 30 MINUTES

I am a big fan of southern fried foods—the crispier and crunchier, the better. Most fried foods take a long time, though, and I don't relish standing in front of the stovetop waiting for my food to be ready. I would much rather throw it in the oven and walk away until the timer chimes—so that's what I do here. The chicken skin gets super crispy, and the meat juicy and tender. Barbecue sauce is a perfect finishing touch.

1 (3- to 4-pound) whole chicken, cut into pieces

1 cup barbecue sauce

1 cup mayonnaise

2 cups cornflake crumbs

1. Preheat the oven to 350°F. Line a baking sheet with parchment paper.

2. Place the chicken pieces on the prepared baking sheet.

3. In a medium bowl, stir together the barbecue sauce and mayonnaise. Spread the mixture on top of the chicken, covering all sides, then sprinkle the chicken with the cornflake crumbs, pressing them in to coat all sides.

4. Bake for 90 minutes or until the chicken is cooked through.

Per serving: Calories: 620; Total fat: 40g; Total carbs: 43g; Fiber: 1g; Sugar: 14g; Protein: 22g; Sodium: 910mg

Honey-Mustard Chicken with Rosemary

MEAT • EASY PREP • FAMILY FAVORITE • G GLUTEN FREE • GF GRAIN FREE • NUT FREE

SERVES 4 TO 5 | PREP TIME: 10 MINUTES | COOK TIME: 45 MINUTES

A recipe does not need to have a long list of ingredients or an elaborate presentation—even (or especially) when guests are coming to dinner. This recipe for honey-mustard chicken with rosemary is a perfect example of something that's easy, tasty, and impressive without much effort. All you really need for a no-fuss "wow" factor is a glossy sauce (check), a crispy skin (check), and some fresh herbs to top it all off. This one hits it out of the park with all three.

1½ pounds chicken thighs (about 5 pieces)

¼ teaspoon salt

⅛ teaspoon freshly ground black pepper

¼ cup honey

¼ cup mustard

4 sprigs rosemary (plus more for serving)

1. Preheat the oven to 350°F.
2. In a large baking dish, season the chicken with the salt and pepper.
3. In a small bowl, whisk together the honey and mustard until smooth.
4. Pour the honey-mustard sauce over the chicken. Place the rosemary sprigs between the chicken pieces.
5. Bake in the oven for 45 minutes or until the chicken is cooked through. Garnish with fresh rosemary.

Ingredient Tip: The honey-mustard sauce tastes amazing spooned over steamed broccoli!

Per serving: Calories: 471; Total fat: 28g; Total carbs: 21g; Fiber: 2g; Sugar: 18g; Protein: 33g; Sodium: 276mg

Falafel-Coated Chicken Fingers

 MEAT ♡ FAMILY FAVORITE ◇ NUT FREE

SERVES 4 TO 5 | PREP TIME: 10 MINUTES | COOK TIME: 10 MINUTES

I love all styles of Israeli food, like shawarma, sabich, and shakshuka, but falafel is definitely top of the list. I like stuffing falafel balls in a pita and loading it up with as many salads and dips that I can fit—the messier the better! I especially love schnitzel and falafel served together with hummus, so I decided to turn it into one dish by coating the chicken in falafel mix. The resulting dish is as delicious as I could have hoped.

4 eggs, whisked together

1 (6.3 ounce) box falafel mix

1½ pounds boneless, skinless chicken breasts, cut into pieces

¼ cup canola oil, for frying

½ cup Classic Hummus (page 14)

1. Place the eggs in a large, shallow dish.
2. Place the falafel mix in a separate large dish.
3. One at a time, dip each chicken piece in the eggs, then in the falafel mixture.
4. Heat 2 tablespoons of oil in a large skillet over medium-high heat. Fry the coated chicken pieces in batches, adding more oil as needed with each batch, until golden brown, about 5 minutes per side.
5. Serve with hummus.

Variation Tip: Create a delicious Middle Eastern spread by placing chicken pieces on a large platter with hummus, tahini, and Israeli salad (diced cucumbers, tomatoes, and red onion, seasoned with olive oil, salt, pepper, and some fresh lemon juice), topped with za'atar and sesame seeds.

Per serving: Calories: 442; Total fat: 12g; Total carbs: 27g; Fiber: 8g; Sugar: 3g; Protein: 54g; Sodium: 998mg

Spinach and Beef Stuffed Shells

 MEAT NUT FREE

SERVES 4 TO 5 | PREP TIME: 15 MINUTES | COOK TIME: 35 MINUTES

If I have to hide vegetables in my kids' food so that they will eat them, I'll do it. I am not above being a sneaky mom in the kitchen. My boys love anything with pasta and these shells are stuffed with ground beef, another win in their eyes. They love eating this dinner so much they don't even seem to notice the spinach. You can stuff these shells with a mixture of ground beef and any vegetable you want to get your kid to eat. Steamed cauliflower mashed into pieces would taste delicious, too.

1 (12-ounce) package jumbo pasta shells

1 pound ground beef

1 cup frozen spinach, thawed

1 (24-ounce) jar marinara sauce

1. Preheat the oven to 350°F.

2. Cook the pasta shells in a large pot of boiling water for 12 minutes. Drain and set aside.

3. Meanwhile, in a large skillet, cook the ground beef, using a spatula to break it into pieces. Add the spinach to the pan and stir to combine.

4. Add three-quarters of the marinara sauce to the beef mixture and stir to combine. Cook for an additional 5 minutes.

5. Stuff the pasta shells with the beef-spinach mixture.

6. In a large baking dish, arrange the stuffed shells and top with the remaining marinara sauce. Bake for 15 to 20 minutes.

Variation Tip: Ground chicken, ground turkey, or meatless veggie crumbles can be used in place of the beef. You can also swap out the spinach for sautéed onions and mushrooms.

Per serving: Calories: 518; Total fat: 10g; Total carbs: 71g; Fiber: 6g; Sugar: 10g; Protein: 35g; Sodium: 982mg

Cheese Pancakes

🥛 DAIRY 🚫 NUT FREE

SERVES 4 TO 5 | PREP TIME: 10 MINUTES | COOK TIME: 20 MINUTES

These cheese pancakes are like quick miniature versions of cheese blintzes. My kids like them just as much, which is a win for me, since these are so much easier to prepare. Simply combine farmer's cheese, flour, sugar, vanilla, and eggs in a bowl, then fry the batter in batches until slightly golden brown, and serve with powdered sugar or fresh strawberry jam for a delicious brunch—or the always-popular breakfast for dinner.

1 pound farmer's cheese, dry cottage cheese, or ricotta cheese

1 cup all-purpose flour

½ cup sugar

6 eggs

1 teaspoon vanilla extract

¼ cup canola oil, for frying

1. In a large mixing bowl, use an electric mixer to combine the farmer's cheese, flour, sugar, eggs, and vanilla.

2. Heat 2 tablespoons of oil in a large skillet and cook the batter in batches (about ¼ cup at a time), adding more oil as needed with each batch, until the pancakes are slightly browned on both sides.

Variation Tip: Serve with strawberry jam. Another option is to add a dash of cinnamon to the batter before cooking.

Per serving: Calories: 486; Total fat: 19g; Total carbs: 53g; Fiber: 1g; Sugar: 30g; Protein: 26g; Sodium: 453mg

GREEK-STYLE STUFFED SALMON *page 87*

Chapter Five
ONE-POT

Lemon Chicken with Rosemary and Thyme

◯ MEAT Ⓖ GLUTEN FREE GF GRAIN FREE ◯ NUT FREE SF SUGAR FREE

SERVES 5 TO 6 | PREP TIME: 5 MINUTES | COOK TIME: 1 HOUR

Fresh, tart lemon slices and sprigs of fragrant rosemary and thyme blend together in this easy and simple all-in-one dish, creating a vibrant flavor that is anything but simple. It is the perfect cozy dinner for gathering around the table. The finished chicken has crispy, spiced skin and remains juicy inside, as the water in the pan prevents the chicken from drying out. The water bath is a tip my mom gave me when I first started cooking back in high school, and I've been using it ever since.

1 small onion, cut into thin half moons

1 lemon, cut into thin rounds

1 small bunch thyme

1 small bunch rosemary

1 (3- to 4-pound) whole chicken, cut into 8 pieces

1 tablespoon olive oil

½ teaspoon salt

¼ teaspoon freshly ground black pepper

½ teaspoon garlic powder

½ teaspoon paprika

½ cup water, or more as needed

1. Preheat the oven to 350°F.

2. In a 9-by-13-inch baking dish, place the onions in an even layer. Layer the lemons on top of the onions, then cover with the thyme and rosemary.

3. Place the chicken pieces on top of the herbs.

4. Drizzle the olive oil on top of the chicken pieces and season with the salt, black pepper, garlic powder, and paprika.

5. Pour water into the baking dish to come up the sides by about an inch.

6. Bake for about an hour or until the juices run clear and the chicken reaches an internal temperature of 165°F. Serve with the juices from the pan.

Per serving: Calories: 303; Total fat: 20g; Total carbs: 2g; Fiber: 0g; Sugar: 1g; Protein: 28g; Sodium: 436mg

Honey-Lime Grilled Chicken

 MEAT EASY PREP NUT FREE

SERVES 4 | PREP TIME: 5 MINUTES | COOK TIME: 15 MINUTES

Some nights (okay, most nights), I crave carbs like pizza and pasta. But there are other times when all I want is a plate piled high with roasted veggies—zucchini, cauliflower, and carrots—with a side of perfectly grilled chicken. This sweet, salty, and citrusy marinade blends together some of my favorite flavors and helps create a delicious glazed chicken with a kick of lime.

¼ cup olive oil

¼ cup soy sauce

Juice of 1 lime, plus additional for serving

3 tablespoons honey

3 garlic cloves, chopped

1 tablespoon chopped fresh ginger

½ teaspoon freshly ground black pepper

4 boneless, skinless chicken breasts

1. In a large zip-top bag, combine the olive oil, soy sauce, lime juice, honey, garlic, ginger, and black pepper.

2. Place the chicken in the bag so the breasts are thoroughly coated. Let marinate in the refrigerator for 30 minutes to an hour.

3. Heat a grill pan over medium-high heat. Remove the chicken from the marinade; discard the marinade. Grill the chicken for about 6 minutes on each side or until the juices run clear.

4. Squeeze fresh lime on top before serving.

Per serving: Calories: 296; Total fat: 14g; Total carbs: 17g; Fiber: 1g; Sugar: 14g; Protein: 27g; Sodium: 975mg

Skillet Lasagna with Mushrooms and Mozzarella

(I) DAIRY (V) VEGETARIAN

SERVES 4 TO 6 | PREP TIME: 10 MINUTES | COOK TIME: 25 MINUTES

While I love a hearty lasagna, I am far from thrilled at the thought of boiling noodles, having to assemble the dish, and then waiting for it to bake. What I love about this recipe is that it has the familiar flavor of the classic, but without the fuss. I cook my veggies, noodles, sauce, and cheese all in one pot. No baking. No mess. This is the perfect weeknight dinner.

1 tablespoon olive oil

1 large yellow onion, diced

8 ounces sliced mushrooms

1 (26-ounce) jar marinara sauce

2 tablespoons tomato paste

1 tablespoon brown sugar

10 lasagna noodles

2½ cups water

1 (8-ounce) mozzarella ball, thinly sliced

Fresh basil, for serving (optional)

1. In a large skillet, heat the oil.

2. Cook the onion until translucent, then add the mushrooms and cook until tender and browned. Add the marinara sauce, tomato paste, and brown sugar and combine well.

3. Break each lasagna noodle into three pieces and add them to the sauce.

4. Add the water to the pan, stirring the noodles so they are covered with water and sauce. Cook until the noodles are softened, about 20 minutes.

5. Add the mozzarella slices on top of the noodles, then cover for an additional 5 minutes or until melted. Serve with fresh basil (if using).

Variation Tip: Swap the mushrooms for spinach, thinly sliced peppers, asparagus, or your favorite veggies. You can also make this a meat dish by adding ground beef to the mushrooms and removing the mozzarella.

Per serving: Calories: 428; Total fat: 17g; Total carbs: 50g; Fiber: 6g; Sugar: 15g; Protein: 24g; Sodium: 837mg

Ginger Chicken and Spinach with Rice

MEAT · **G GLUTEN FREE** · **NUT FREE** · **SF SUGAR FREE**

SERVES 4 TO 6 | PREP TIME: 10 MINUTES | COOK TIME: 50 MINUTES

This is a wonderfully savory one-pot dish that makes a flavorful meal with easy preparation and even easier cleanup. I love a strong ginger flavor, but if you don't, simply leave it out or replace it with your favorite spices. You can also use mushrooms and bell pepper strips in place of the spinach and rice, or sub in cauliflower, broccoli florets, or kale.

2 tablespoons olive oil

1 small onion, diced

1 teaspoon salt

¼ teaspoon freshly ground black pepper

½ teaspoon garlic powder

½ teaspoon ground ginger

1 pound boneless, skinless chicken breast (about 4 pieces), cubed

1 cup uncooked rice

2 cups vegetable or chicken stock

2 cups chopped spinach (fresh or frozen)

1. In a large pot, heat the olive oil and cook the onion in the oil until golden. Season with the salt, pepper, garlic powder, and ginger.

2. Add the chicken pieces and cook until the chicken is no longer pink.

3. Add the rice, stock, and spinach to the pot, cover, and simmer until the liquid is absorbed and the rice is cooked, 30 to 45 minutes.

Per serving: Calories: 381; Total fat: 10g; Total carbs: 40g; Fiber: 1g; Sugar: 1g; Protein: 32g; Sodium: 935mg

Chicken Cacciatore

 MEAT   NUT FREE   SF SUGAR FREE

SERVES 4 TO 6 | PREP TIME: 10 MINUTES | COOK TIME: 1 HOUR

Chicken cacciatore is a classic Italian dish—basically just chicken prepared "hunter style" with chunks of tomatoes, onions, fresh herbs, red or white wine, mushrooms, and strips of red bell peppers. Once prepared, it is often served over thick egg noodles. This one-pot version will become a family favorite, as it is perfect for feeding a hungry crowd or satisfying your cravings for a warm, comforting meal.

¼ cup all-purpose flour

2 teaspoons freshly ground black pepper, divided

2 teaspoons salt, divided

1 (3- to 4-pound) whole chicken, cut into pieces

1 tablespoon olive oil

1 onion, diced

3 garlic cloves, chopped

1 pound cremini mushrooms, sliced

1 red bell pepper, diced

1 (28-ounce) can crushed tomatoes

½ cup red wine

1 teaspoon chopped fresh oregano

1 bay leaf

Fresh parsley, chopped, for serving (optional)

1. In a large mixing bowl, combine the flour, 1 teaspoon of black pepper, and 1 teaspoon of salt.

2. Dredge the chicken pieces in the flour mixture.

3. In a large skillet, heat the oil over medium heat and brown the chicken pieces, about 5 minutes each side. Remove the chicken from the skillet and set aside.

4. Add the onion, garlic, mushrooms, and red bell pepper to the skillet and cook until tender.

5. Add the crushed tomatoes, red wine, chopped oregano, and bay leaf to the skillet. Season with the remaining 1 teaspoon of black pepper and 1 teaspoon of salt. Stir and bring to a boil.

6. Return the chicken to the sauce, lower the heat, and cook for about 45 minutes or until the chicken is cooked through. Remove the bay leaf before serving and garnish with chopped fresh parsley (if using).

Per serving: Calories: 448; Total fat: 22g; Total carbs: 25g; Fiber: 7g; Sugar: 13g; Protein: 35g; Sodium: 1123mg

Cajun Sausage Rice Bowl

 MEAT  GLUTEN FREE NUT FREE SUGAR FREE

SERVES 4 TO 6 | PREP TIME: 10 MINUTES | COOK TIME: 45 MINUTES

There is nothing I enjoy more than ending the day with a deliciously easy and hearty meal. Carbs were created to make you feel all warm and cozy inside, and rice is at the top of the comfort food list for me. Cooked together with vibrant spices and savory slices of sausage and pepper, this one-pot dish is full of flavor in every creamy, comforting bite.

1 tablespoon olive oil

1 onion, diced

1 large red bell pepper, chopped

12 ounces sausage, cut into rounds

2 teaspoons Cajun seasoning

1 teaspoon salt

1½ cups uncooked brown rice

1 (32-ounce) carton (or 4 cups) reduced-sodium chicken stock

1. In a large skillet over medium-high heat, heat the oil and sauté the onion and pepper until tender.

2. Add the sausage rounds to the pan and cook until the edges are slightly crispy, about 5 minutes, stirring every so often so they don't stick to the pan. Add the Cajun seasoning and salt.

3. Add the rice and chicken stock and combine well. Cover and simmer on medium-low heat until the liquid is absorbed, 30 to 45 minutes. Fluff with a fork before serving.

Variation Tip: If you like, add some chopped fresh cilantro or parsley for color and extra flavor. You can also swap out the sausage for salami, hot dogs, or boneless, skinless chicken.

Per serving: Calories: 519; Total fat: 21g; Total carbs: 60g; Fiber: 3g; Sugar: 3g; Protein: 22g; Sodium: 1566mg

Apple Cider Chicken with Apples and Pears

⬤ MEAT Ⓖ GLUTEN FREE ⒼⒻ GRAIN FREE ◯ NUT FREE

SERVES 4 TO 6 | PREP TIME: 10 MINUTES | COOK TIME: 30 MINUTES

I like to think that the easiest recipes can also be the most delicious ones, and this dish proves it. With just a few simple ingredients, you can cook up a mouthwatering meal that everyone will enjoy. Tart apples and sweet pears cook together while the chicken soaks up the delicious, deep taste of the apple cider to make for a wholesome and nurturing one-pot dish that is full of autumnal flavor.

2 tablespoons olive oil, divided

1 small onion, thinly sliced

1 pound (about 4 pieces) boneless, skinless chicken breasts

1 large apple, peeled and thinly sliced

1 large pear, peeled and thinly sliced

1 cup apple cider

1 tablespoon apple cider vinegar

1. In a large skillet, heat 1 tablespoon of olive oil over medium heat and cook the onion until translucent.

2. Add the chicken pieces and cook until they are no longer pink.

3. Remove the chicken from the heat and set aside, wrapping it in aluminum foil to keep warm.

4. Add the remaining 1 tablespoon of olive oil to the pan, then add the apple and pear slices and cook until tender.

5. Combine the apple cider with the apple cider vinegar, pour it into the pan, and bring to a boil.

6. Lower the heat and return the chicken pieces to the pan. Cook for an additional 5 minutes and serve.

Per serving: Calories: 266; Total fat: 9g; Total carbs: 22g; Fiber: 3g; Sugar: 17g; Protein: 27g; Sodium: 79mg

Spiced Chicken over Pierogis with Honey and Soy Sauce

MEAT · NUT FREE

SERVES 5 TO 6 | PREP TIME: 10 MINUTES | COOK TIME: 1 HOUR 30 MINUTES

This recipe is a staple on my weekly dinner menu for two simple reasons: One, it is ridiculously easy to prepare, and two, the flavor is fantastic. The potato pierogis soak up the soy sauce–honey mixture, creating tender, delicious bites of potato and dough under perfectly cooked chicken. I have also made this with a quick swap of thinly sliced potatoes in place of the pierogis.

1 (14-ounce) package nondairy potato pierogis

1 (3- to 4-pound) whole chicken, cut into 8 pieces

1 tablespoon olive oil

½ teaspoon garlic powder

½ teaspoon salt

½ teaspoon paprika

¼ teaspoon freshly ground black pepper

1 tablespoon honey

1 tablespoon soy sauce

¼ cup water

1. Preheat the oven to 350°F.

2. In a 9-by-13-inch baking dish, arrange the pierogis and top them with the chicken pieces. Drizzle with the olive oil, and season with the garlic powder, salt, paprika, and black pepper.

3. Drizzle the honey and soy sauce over the top, and pour the water into the baking dish.

4. Cover the baking dish with aluminum foil and bake for 1 hour, then remove the foil and cook for an additional 20 to 30 minutes or until the chicken is cooked through.

Per serving: Calories: 452; Total fat: 23g; Total carbs: 28g; Fiber: 1g; Sugar: 5g; Protein: 33g; Sodium: 943mg

Tilapia Baked with Cumin, Tomatoes, and Potatoes

P PAREVE **G** GLUTEN FREE **GF** GRAIN FREE **⊘** NUT FREE

SERVES 4 TO 6 | PREP TIME: 10 MINUTES | COOK TIME: 20 MINUTES

In this quick bake, perfectly seasoned tilapia cooks over a flavorful blend of thinly sliced onions, tomatoes, and potatoes until it's melt-in-your-mouth tender. This dish can be cooked using a whole fish or fillets—I find it easier to cook and serve individual fillets. If cooking the whole tilapia, increase the cook time to 45 minutes.

⅛ cup olive oil

⅛ teaspoon freshly ground black pepper

¼ teaspoon salt

¼ teaspoon paprika

¼ teaspoon ground cumin

2 pounds tilapia fillets

1 large onion, cut into thin rounds

1 large tomato, cut into thin rounds

4 small gold potatoes, peeled and cut into thin rounds

1. Preheat the oven to 400°F.

2. In a large mixing bowl, combine the olive oil, black pepper, salt, paprika, and cumin.

3. Dip the tilapia fillets in the seasoning mixture to coat them on both sides.

4. In a 9-by-13-inch baking dish, layer the onion, tomato, and potato slices, then place the seasoned tilapia on top.

5. Bake uncovered for 20 minutes or until the fish flakes easily with a fork.

Per serving: Calories: 395; Total fat: 9g; Total carbs: 35g; Fiber: 5g; Sugar: 4g; Protein: 46g; Sodium: 241mg

Easy Marinated Pepper Steak

 MEAT  NUT FREE

SERVES 4 TO 6 | PREP TIME: 10 MINUTES | COOK TIME: 20 MINUTES

Fewer pots on the stove mean fewer pots to clean post–dinner hustle, and that is an equation that works for me. In this recipe, strips of flank steak cook with onions and peppers until tender and delicious, and the sweet soy marinade creates a delectably sticky glaze that cooks in minutes. My boys love steak and I enjoy a good savory sauce, so this dish is one that both mom and the kiddos will devour in equal measure.

¼ cup soy sauce

½ cup water

1 tablespoon rice vinegar

1 teaspoon crushed fresh or frozen ginger

2 teaspoons crushed fresh or frozen garlic

1 pound flank steak, cut into thin strips

2 tablespoons olive oil

1 onion, thinly sliced

1 red bell pepper, cut into thin strips

1 teaspoon cornstarch

1. In a large bowl, combine the soy sauce, water, rice vinegar, ginger, and garlic. Place half of the marinade in a large zip-top plastic bag; set aside the remainder.

2. Place the steak in the bag with the marinade, seal, and set aside to marinate for 20 to 30 minutes.

3. In a large skillet, heat the oil. Cook the onion and bell pepper until tender. Remove the steak from the marinade (discard the bag of marinade) and add the steak to the pan; cook until browned on all sides.

4. Whisk the cornstarch into the bowl of reserved marinade.

5. Move the steak and veggies to one side of the skillet and pour the reserved marinade into the center. Stir over medium heat until the sauce thickens, then mix in all the ingredients in the pan so the sauce is evenly distributed.

Per serving: Calories: 292; Total fat: 17g; Total carbs: 7g; Fiber: 1g; Sugar: 3g; Protein: 26g; Sodium: 901mg

Shakshuka with Sausage

MEAT **G** GLUTEN FREE **GF** GRAIN FREE **NUT FREE** **SF** SUGAR FREE

SERVES 4 TO 6 | PREP TIME: 10 MINUTES | COOK TIME: 20 TO 30 MINUTES

If I had to choose just one brunch food to eat, it would be shakshuka. Soft, runny eggs cooked in a flavorful tomato base with onions and garlic and peppers—it is both mouthwatering and filling at the same time. In this version, I add savory bites of sausage to the tomato sauce with the eggs. Once you try it, you'll find yourself craving it morning, noon, and night.

1 tablespoon olive oil

1 onion, diced

1 red bell pepper, diced

1 yellow bell pepper, diced

3 garlic cloves, chopped

4 sausages (1 pound), cut into thin rounds

1 (16-ounce) jar tomato sauce

½ teaspoon salt

¼ teaspoon freshly ground black pepper

½ teaspoon sweet red paprika

¼ teaspoon ground cumin

5 eggs

Chopped fresh parsley or cilantro, for serving

1. In a large skillet over medium-high heat, heat the olive oil. Add the onion, peppers, and garlic and cook until the veggies are tender. Add the sausage rounds and cook until they are slightly browned, then stir in the tomato sauce, salt, black pepper, paprika, and cumin.

2. Gently crack the eggs open one at a time, placing them in different spots on top of the sauce, cover the skillet, reduce the heat to low, and simmer for 10 to 15 minutes or until the eggs are set yet still slightly runny.

3. Garnish with chopped parsley and serve.

Per serving: Calories: 432; Total fat: 30g; Total carbs: 15g; Fiber: 3g; Sugar: 9g; Protein: 26g; Sodium: 1295mg

Greek-Style Stuffed Salmon

D DAIRY **G** GLUTEN FREE **GF** GRAIN FREE **⊘** NUT FREE **SF** SUGAR FREE

SERVES 4 | PREP TIME: 10 MINUTES | COOK TIME: 15 MINUTES

With this quick recipe, you get your main dish and salad combo all in one. The vegetables cook perfectly with the salmon, the feta cheese melts in your mouth, and the dill dressing adds just the right amount of flavor. It is a really tasty and easy weeknight dinner, but it can also be impressive enough for entertaining. Serve it with a side of jasmine rice or mashed cauliflower to finish off the plate.

1 tablespoon freshly squeezed lemon juice

3 tablespoons olive oil

2 garlic cloves, crushed

1 tablespoon chopped fresh dill

½ teaspoon salt

¼ teaspoon freshly ground black pepper

2 pounds salmon fillet, cut into 4 equal pieces

4 Campari tomatoes on the vine, cut in half

1 small red onion, sliced thinly

⅓ cup pitted Kalamata olives, thinly sliced

¼ cup crumbled feta cheese

1. Preheat the oven to 450°F. Line a baking sheet with parchment paper.

2. In a small bowl, whisk together the lemon juice, olive oil, garlic, dill, salt, and pepper.

3. Place the salmon on the prepared baking sheet. Using a sharp paring knife, make slits along the length of the salmon, making sure you don't cut all the way through the fish. You can slice through the side or top of the fish.

4. Brush the salmon with the olive oil–dill mixture, then stuff the slits in the fish with the tomato halves, onion slices, and olives. Top with the crumbled feta.

5. Bake for 12 minutes or until the salmon flakes easily with a fork.

Per serving: Calories: 460; Total fat: 32g; Total carbs: 8g; Fiber: 2g; Sugar: 4g; Protein: 36g; Sodium: 599mg

Dairy-Free Chicken Alfredo with Broccoli

 MEAT **SF** SUGAR FREE

SERVES 5 TO 6 | PREP TIME: 10 MINUTES | COOK TIME: 35 MINUTES

This creamy sauce tastes so good, you would swear there is heavy cream in it somewhere. Instead, the roux that forms the base of this cheesy sauce is made with Earth Balance spread and soy milk. Since it's dairy free, you can add in chunks of delicious seasoned chicken—a kosher foodie's dream come true.

1 pound boneless, skinless chicken breasts

3 tablespoons olive oil, divided

1 teaspoon salt, divided

¾ teaspoon freshly ground black pepper, divided

1 head broccoli, roughly chopped into florets

2 tablespoons Earth Balance

2 tablespoons all-purpose flour

2 cups plain unsweetened soy milk or almond milk

½ teaspoon garlic powder

¼ teaspoon ground nutmeg

1. In a baking dish, place the chicken breasts and rub them on all sides with 1 tablespoon of olive oil, ½ teaspoon of salt, and ¼ teaspoon of black pepper.

2. Heat the remaining 2 tablespoons of oil in a large pot over medium heat and cook the chicken breasts until no longer pink, 8 to 10 minutes per side. Add the broccoli florets and cook until they are bright green and softened, about 5 minutes.

3. Transfer the chicken to a cutting board and scoop the broccoli into a bowl. Let the chicken stand for several minutes, then cut it into thin strips or cubes.

4. In the same pot, melt the Earth Balance over medium-high heat. Whisk in the flour until a thick paste forms, then stream in the soy milk and whisk until smooth. Continue whisking until thickened. Season with the remaining ½ teaspoon of salt and ½ teaspoon of black pepper, garlic powder, and nutmeg.

5. Add the cooked chicken and broccoli to the sauce; mix well before serving.

Per serving: Calories: 299; Total fat: 16g; Total carbs: 14g; Fiber: 3g; Sugar: 5g; Protein: 27g; Sodium: 647mg

Matzo Ball–Topped Chicken Pot Pie

 MEAT   NUT FREE

SERVES 5 TO 6 | PREP TIME: 10 MINUTES, PLUS 10 MINUTES CHILLING TIME | COOK TIME: 30 MINUTES

When you hear matzo balls, you might instantly think of chicken noodle soup, but that is not the only way you can enjoy this classic Jewish food. I really like giving traditional recipes a modern makeover, and this dish does just that by baking matzo balls on top of creamy chicken pot pie filling. The nice, thick topping makes for the ultimate comfort-food mashup.

4 eggs

2 tablespoons vegetable oil

2 (4.5-ounce) packets matzo ball mix

1 tablespoon olive oil

1 pound boneless, skinless chicken breast, cut into bite-size cubes

1 (12-ounce) package mixed frozen peas and carrots

3½ cups vegetable stock divided

⅓ cup all-purpose flour

1. Preheat the oven to 350°F.

2. To prepare the matzo balls: In a medium bowl, whisk together the eggs and vegetable oil. Add both packets of matzo ball mix and stir with a fork until the batter is well combined. Refrigerate for 10 minutes.

3. Meanwhile, in a large ovenproof skillet over medium-high heat, heat the olive oil. Add the chicken pieces and cook until they are no longer pink, 5 to 7 minutes. Add the frozen peas and carrots and stir until they are heated through. Add 3 cups of vegetable stock and the flour. Reduce the heat to medium and stir until the sauce thickens.

4. Remove the matzo ball mixture from the refrigerator. Portion out the batter using an ice cream scoop, and use wet hands to form each piece into a ball. Place the matzo balls on top of the chicken mixture in the skillet.

5. Pour the remaining ½ cup of vegetable stock over the matzo balls.

6. Bake for 12 to 15 minutes or until the matzo balls are firm.

Per serving: Calories: 466; Total fat: 13g; Total carbs: 57g; Fiber: 3g; Sugar: 3g; Protein: 31g; Sodium: 926mg

Crispy Tofu Parmesan

D DAIRY **⊘** NUT FREE **SF** SUGAR FREE **V** VEGETARIAN

SERVES 4 | PREP TIME: 10 MINUTES, PLUS 20 MINUTES FOR DRAINING THE TOFU | COOK TIME: 25 MINUTES

There are certain foods I have always wanted to taste, but they were always off-limits. Chicken Parmesan is one of those foods—it always looked so delicious. Once I started cooking tofu with a crispy coating, similar to schnitzel, I realized I finally had my chance to create a kosher version of chicken Parmesan. While it's not chicken, it still has the same crispy coating with layers of sauce and melted cheese, and it is close enough (and tasty enough!) to satisfy my craving.

1 (12-ounce) package extra-firm tofu

2 eggs

1 cup cornflake crumbs

2 cups marinara sauce

4 (½-inch-thick) slices mozzarella cheese

½ cup grated Parmesan

1. Preheat the oven to 400°F. Line a 9-by-13-inch baking dish with parchment paper.

2. Drain the tofu, wrap it in paper towels, and leave it on the counter to drain for 20 minutes. Pat it dry with clean paper towels.

3. Cut the tofu in half across the middle to make two thinner pieces, then cut each half horizontally to make 4 thick rectangles.

4. In a shallow bowl, whisk the eggs. Place the cornflake crumbs on a plate.

5. Coat the tofu patties in the egg, then dip them in the cornflake crumbs, pressing to coat them on all sides.

6. Transfer the coated tofu to the prepared baking dish and bake for 15 minutes or until slightly crispy.

7. Remove the baking dish from the oven and transfer the tofu to a plate. Spread half of the marinara sauce evenly in the baking dish, then return the tofu to the dish. Pour the remaining sauce on top of the tofu, top with the mozzarella, and sprinkle with the Parmesan. Bake for 5 to 10 minutes or until the cheese has melted.

Per serving: Calories: 335; Total fat: 20g; Total carbs: 19g; Fiber: 8g; Sugar: 9g; Protein: 23g; Sodium: 978mg

Meatless Cheese Taco Cups

 DAIRY NUT FREE **V** VEGETARIAN

MAKES 24 CUPS | PREP TIME: 5 MINUTES | COOK TIME: 20 MINUTES

These meatless taco cups stuffed with Mexican-seasoned veggie crumbles and topped with melted Cheddar and salsa are so tasty—and perfect for dinner or a party appetizer. Kids and adults both adore the bite-size portions and melted cheese. Once baked, the veggie crumbles have a very similar texture to ground beef and really taste like taco meat.

Nonstick cooking spray

24 wonton wrappers (thawed if frozen)

1 (12-ounce) package Mexican-style veggie crumbles (such as Lightlife Smart Ground)

1 (16-ounce) jar salsa

8 ounces Cheddar cheese, shredded

1. Preheat the oven to 325°F. Spray the cups of a 24-cup mini muffin pan with nonstick cooking spray.

2. Place one wonton wrapper in each cup, pressing down so it sticks. Bake the wrappers for 10 minutes (the edges should be slightly browned).

3. Remove the muffin pan from the oven and keep the wonton cups in the pan. Layer each wonton cup with 1 tablespoon of veggie crumbles, 1 teaspoon of salsa, and 1 teaspoon of shredded Cheddar cheese.

4. Return the pan to the oven and bake for another 10 minutes, until the cheese is nice and bubbly.

Per serving (1 cup): Calories: 154; Total fat: 4g; Total carbs: 21g; Fiber: 2g; Sugar: 1g; Protein: 9g; Sodium: 415mg

PERSIAN GREEN BEAN STEW *page 101*

Chapter Six

SLOW COOKER & PRESSURE COOKER

Butternut Squash Quinoa Stew

P PAREVE **G** GLUTEN FREE **N** NUT FREE **SF** SUGAR FREE **V** VEGETARIAN

SERVES 4 TO 6 | PREP TIME: 5 MINUTES | COOK TIME: 3 TO 5 HOURS

This dish pairs sweet chunks of butternut squash with hearty quinoa, creating a filling meal that is full of flavor and makes your kitchen smell amazing. The coconut milk adds a delicious creaminess, while the chickpeas add texture to the smooth and fluffy quinoa. This is a wholesome, meatless meal that is satisfying and simple to prepare, thanks to the slow cooker. You combine the ingredients and then walk away and let it do the work for you. The final result is a savory stew you can't wait to dig in to.

1 butternut squash, peeled, seeded, and diced

2 small zucchini, chopped

2 garlic cloves, chopped

1 tablespoon minced fresh ginger

1 onion, diced

1 (15.5-ounce) can chickpeas (garbanzo beans), rinsed and drained

1½ cups uncooked quinoa

1¼ cups vegetable stock

1 (14-ounce) can coconut milk

1 (14.5-ounce) can diced tomatoes

½ teaspoon ground cumin

½ teaspoon ground turmeric

¼ teaspoon freshly ground black pepper

½ teaspoon ground coriander

1. In a slow cooker, combine the butternut squash, zucchini, garlic, ginger, onion, chickpeas, quinoa, stock, coconut milk, tomatoes, cumin, turmeric, pepper, and coriander and mix well.

2. Cover and cook on High for 3 to 5 hours. It's that simple!

Per serving: Calories: 689; Total fat: 30g; Total carbs: 90g; Fiber: 17g; Sugar: 15g; Protein: 22g; Sodium: 328mg

Slow Cooker Beef Stew

 MEAT NUT FREE

SERVES 4 TO 6 | PREP TIME: 20 MINUTES | COOK TIME: 4 TO 6 HOURS

After a long day out, there is no greater feeling than coming back to a delicious, ready-to-eat home-cooked meal. Such is the gift of the slow cooker. This thick and hearty stew is flavorful and simple. Yes, it does require a little prep work, but trust me—it's worth it. Browning the meat first creates tender pieces of beef that are extra rich and bring out the best flavor of the stew.

⅓ cup all-purpose flour

¼ teaspoon freshly ground black pepper

1 pound cubed beef stew meat

2 tablespoons olive oil

1 large onion, chopped

1 pound green beans, trimmed

6 small carrots, peeled and chopped

2 large Yukon Gold potatoes, chopped

1 teaspoon brown sugar

1 cube beef bouillon

1 (14.5-ounce) can diced tomatoes, plain or herb-flavored, with their juices

2 bay leaves

4 cups water

1. In a large bowl, mix together the flour and black pepper. Add the beef and toss to coat.

2. In a large skillet over medium-high heat, heat the olive oil. Add the beef in small batches and brown it on all sides, 15 to 20 minutes total for all the meat. Transfer the browned beef to a slow cooker.

3. To the slow cooker, add the onion, green beans, carrots, potatoes, brown sugar, bouillon cube, tomatoes, bay leaves, and water and mix well.

4. Cover and cook on High for 4 to 6 hours or on Low for 8 to 10 hours.

5. Remove the bay leaves before serving.

Variation Tip: If desired, you can cook this recipe in a Dutch oven. Preheat the oven to 300°F. Brown the meat in the Dutch oven, then add all the remaining ingredients, cover, and transfer to the oven for 4 to 5 hours.

Per serving: Calories: 501; Total fat: 23g; Total carbs: 48g; Fiber: 10g; Sugar: 12g; Protein: 32g; Sodium: 493mg

Shredded Salsa Chicken

MEAT   G GLUTEN FREE   GF GRAIN FREE   NUT FREE

SERVES 4 TO 6 | PREP TIME: 5 MINUTES | COOK TIME: 6 HOURS

I love a good shredded chicken dish, and this one doesn't disappoint, with the delicious flavor combination of salsa, cilantro, and a hint of lime. Enjoy it on a baked potato, with long-grain rice, or stuffed in a burrito with black beans, Pico de Gallo (page 139), and guacamole.

4 boneless, skinless chicken breasts

1 (16-ounce) jar chunky salsa

1 (1.25-ounce) package taco seasoning

1 cup chicken stock

1 tablespoon freshly squeezed lime juice

¼ cup chopped fresh cilantro

1. In a slow cooker, combine the chicken, salsa, taco seasoning, stock, lime juice, and cilantro.

2. Cover and cook on Low for 6 hours.

3. Transfer the chicken to a large cutting board and shred it using two forks, then return it to the slow cooker and mix it into the sauce.

Variation Tip: Serve the shredded chicken and some of the juices from the slow cooker over rice with freshly chopped cilantro, in tortillas or taco shells with guacamole, or in a taco bowl with rice, beans, corn, and avocado.

Per serving: Calories: 182; Total fat: 3g; Total carbs: 10g; Fiber: 2g; Sugar: 4g; Protein: 30g; Sodium: 988mg

Lemon Chicken with Vegetables

 MEAT GLUTEN FREE **GF** GRAIN FREE ⊘ NUT FREE **SF** SUGAR FREE

SERVES 4 TO 6 | PREP TIME: 20 MINUTES | COOK TIME: 8 HOURS

My brother-in-law Chaim gave me this simple slow cooker recipe in which a whole chicken slow cooks with zesty lemon and garlic over a bed of hearty vegetables. The result is a pot of tender chicken, potatoes, carrots, onion, and celery—total comfort food. When I think of enjoying a cozy meal with loved ones, this is what I want to serve.

1 (3- to 4-pound) whole chicken

1 lemon, cut in half

6 garlic cloves

2 tablespoons olive oil

1 teaspoon salt

½ teaspoon freshly ground black pepper

1 teaspoon garlic powder

1 teaspoon onion powder

1½ pounds petite potatoes, cut in half

1 (12-ounce) bag baby carrots

1 head celery, trimmed and roughly chopped

10 ounces pearl onions, skins removed

¼ cup chicken stock

1. Stuff the cavity of the chicken with the lemon halves and garlic cloves, then tie the legs together with kitchen twine. (If you don't have kitchen twine, don't worry about tying the legs together.)

2. Drizzle the olive oil over the chicken and rub it on all sides with the salt, black pepper, garlic powder, and onion powder.

3. In a slow cooker, place a thin layer of potatoes, carrots, celery, and onions just to elevate the chicken off the bottom of the inner pot. Place the chicken on top and pour in the stock. Add the remaining vegetables until the pot is full. Cover and cook on Low for 8 hours.

4. Transfer the chicken to a cutting board; remove and discard the lemon and garlic in its cavity. Peel off and discard the chicken skin, and remove the bones.

5. Return the boned chicken pieces to the slow cooker and serve with the vegetables and broth.

Per serving: Calories: 637; Total fat: 31g; Total carbs: 50g; Fiber: 10g; Sugar: 11g; Protein: 40g; Sodium: 934mg

Sweet and Sour Meatballs

 MEAT FAMILY FAVORITE ⬡ NUT FREE

SERVES 4 TO 6 | PREP TIME: 10 MINUTES | COOK TIME: 6 TO 8 HOURS

Thick marinara, tart cranberry sauce, and sweet brown sugar cook together in this family-favorite meatball recipe. My boys request this recipe weekly. Although this is not a traditional Italian-style sauce, the meatballs are great with spaghetti and they love to slurp up the sauce one noodle (and meatball) at a time. This dish is perfect for feeding crowds, since the recipe only has a few ingredients and you can easily double it to cook a larger batch.

1 pound ground beef (or turkey)

2 eggs

⅔ cup breadcrumbs

1 (26-ounce) jar marinara sauce

1 (16-ounce) can jellied cranberry sauce

2 tablespoons light brown sugar

1. In a large bowl, mix together the ground beef, eggs, and breadcrumbs; shape the mixture into tablespoon-size balls.

2. In a slow cooker, combine the marinara sauce, cranberry sauce, and brown sugar. Add the meatballs, cover, and cook on Low for 6 to 8 hours.

Per serving: Calories: 474; Total fat: 11g; Total carbs: 67g; Fiber: 5g; Sugar: 41g; Protein: 29g; Sodium: 948mg

Slow Cooker Cholent
(Beef and Barley Stew)

 MEAT  NUT FREE **SF** SUGAR FREE

SERVES 6 TO 8 | PREP TIME: 10 MINUTES | COOK TIME: 17 HOURS

Cholent is a classic Jewish dish served on Shabbat. It is a slow-cooked (over 17 hours!) stew of meat and potatoes fortified with a blend of beans and barley. On Shabbat, active cooking is not allowed, so cholent is a popular choice—a delicious warm meal that is prepared and cooked before sundown on Friday and finishes overnight in the slow cooker until Shabbat afternoon lunch. If shopping in a kosher market, you will likely find a premade mix of cholent beans; but if you can't find it premixed, use a simple combination of dried kidney beans, navy beans, and pinto beans.

5 medium russet potatoes, peeled and cut into chunks

2 pounds cubed beef stew meat

1 (16-ounce) bag pearled barley

1 cup dried cholent beans (kidney beans, navy beans, and pinto beans)

1 onion, peeled

1 tablespoon canola oil

2 teaspoons salt

2 teaspoons freshly ground black pepper

2 teaspoons garlic powder

2 teaspoons paprika

1. In a slow cooker, place the potatoes, then the meat, barley, beans, and onion. Drizzle in the oil and season liberally with the salt, black pepper, garlic powder, and paprika. Fill the pot about three-quarters full with water.

2. Cover and cook on High for 2 to 3 hours, then set the slow cooker to Low and allow it to cook until lunchtime the following day (about 14 more hours).

Variation Tip: You can add eggs (in their shells) to the pot to slowly cook with the cholent. You can also add barbecue sauce or ketchup to the seasoning mix for an extra punch of flavor.

Per serving: Calories: 740; Total fat: 12g; Total carbs: 109g; Fiber: 22g; Sugar: 4g; Protein: 51g; Sodium: 884mg

Instant Pot® Butternut Squash Soup

P PAREVE **G** GLUTEN FREE **GF** GRAIN FREE **V** VEGAN

SERVES 6 TO 8 | PREP TIME: 20 MINUTES | COOK TIME: 20 MINUTES

Butternut squash soup is always delicious, and it takes only minutes to cook in a pressure cooker. While the soup cooks, I like to prepare one of my favorite toppings to serve with it: Parmesan-coated popcorn! If serving this soup with a dairy meal, this topping is a must. Prepare popcorn as you normally do, then add some olive oil (or melted butter!) and quickly toss it with some shredded Parmesan cheese.

1 tablespoon olive oil

1 onion, diced

2 carrots, peeled and diced

1 butternut squash, peeled, seeded, and cubed

1 teaspoon salt

½ teaspoon freshly ground black pepper

5 cups vegetable stock

1. On an electric pressure cooker, such as an Instant Pot, select Sauté, heat the oil, and cook the onion in the oil until tender, 3 to 5 minutes. Add the carrots and butternut squash, season with the salt and pepper, and pour in the stock. Close and seal the Instant Pot, set the pressure to High, and cook for 15 minutes.

2. When the cooking is finished, allow the pressure to release naturally for about 10 minutes. Then manually release any remaining pressure.

3. Open the Instant Pot and use an immersion blender to purée the soup.

Variation Tip: Swap out the onion for leeks, or add two green apples in place of the carrots for a sweet flavor. Add a pinch of ground coriander and cinnamon to the vegetables before cooking for added richness.

Per serving: Calories: 131; Total fat: 4g; Total carbs: 21g; Fiber: 4g; Sugar: 5g; Protein: 6g; Sodium: 944mg

Persian Green Bean Stew

MEAT G GLUTEN FREE GF GRAIN FREE NUT FREE SF SUGAR FREE

SERVES 4 TO 6 | PREP TIME: 15 MINUTES | COOK TIME: 30 MINUTES

My neighbor, James, is a talented cook. He cooks gourmet meals from scratch without breaking a sweat. Since I like to take it easy in the kitchen, I asked him to share one of his favorite Instant Pot® recipes—but make it super simple. His mom, Diane, raised him on traditional Middle Eastern foods, and this recipe features a simplified version of a traditional Persian dish called beef khoresh. It is a savory stew of meat and beans cooked in a mix of tomato sauce, tomato paste, and spices—a really delicious and filling meal when served over a plate of rice.

2 tablespoons olive oil

1 medium white onion, thinly sliced

1 pound cubed beef stew meat

1 teaspoon salt

¼ teaspoon freshly ground black pepper

½ teaspoon garlic powder

½ teaspoon ground cumin

1 pound green beans, trimmed

2 (16-ounce) cans tomato sauce

2 tablespoons tomato paste

1 bay leaf

1. On an Instant Pot, select Sauté, heat the oil, and add the onion, beef, salt, pepper, garlic powder, and cumin. Cook, stirring constantly, until the meat is browned and the onion is tender, about 5 minutes.

2. Add the green beans, tomato sauce, tomato paste, and bay leaf. Close and seal the Instant Pot, select the Stew setting, and cook for 30 minutes.

3. Once the cooking is done, allow the Instant Pot to release pressure naturally. Remove the bay leaf before serving.

Ingredient Tip: Add two or three dried lemons for an authentic Persian-flavored stew.

Per serving: Calories: 330; Total fat: 14g; Total carbs: 25g; Fiber: 8g; Sugar: 13g; Protein: 30g; Sodium: 1432mg

Instant Pot® Brisket

 MEAT NUT FREE

SERVES 4 TO 6 | PREP TIME: 20 MINUTES | COOK TIME: 1 HOUR 30 MINUTES

My neighbor James was kind enough to share another successful Instant Pot recipe with me, this one for no-fuss brisket. It cooks (in beer!) over carrots and potatoes until the meat is soft and shreds easily with a fork. Serve it in a number of delicious ways: over a plate of creamy mashed potatoes, on tortillas with Pico de Gallo (page 139), or simply with the carrots and potatoes for a wholesome and tasty dinner.

1 teaspoon salt

¼ teaspoon freshly ground black pepper

½ teaspoon garlic powder

½ teaspoon paprika

1 (3-pound) second-cut beef brisket

2 tablespoons olive oil

1 onion, thinly sliced

2 (12-ounce) cans or bottles beer

2 tablespoons barbecue sauce, plus ⅓ cup (optional), divided

1 cup baby carrots

1½ pounds baby potatoes

Per serving: Calories: 481;
Total fat: 18g; Total carbs: 21g;
Fiber: 4g; Sugar: 2g;
Protein: 50g; Sodium: 414mg

1. In a small bowl, combine the salt, pepper, garlic powder, and paprika. Rub the spice mix over the brisket. (If you have time, let the seasoned brisket rest in the refrigerator overnight for an extra-rich flavor.)

2. On an Instant Pot, select Sauté, heat the olive oil, and brown the brisket on all sides; remove the brisket and set aside.

3. Add the onion to the Instant Pot and cook until tender, 3 to 5 minutes, then stir in the beer and 2 tablespoons of barbecue sauce and return the brisket to the pot, along with the carrots and potatoes.

4. Close and seal the Instant Pot, then select the Meat setting on high pressure for 80 minutes.

5. Once cooking is finished, allow the pot to naturally release the pressure. Transfer the brisket to a cutting board and shred it with two forks. Mix the remaining ⅓ cup of barbecue sauce with the shredded brisket (if using).

Ingredient Tip: Use second-cut brisket over first, since the increased fat content creates a more tender cut of meat. You can also use chuck roast for an alternate dish with similar flavors.

Chicken Marsala

 MEAT NUT FREE SUGAR FREE

SERVES 4 TO 6 | PREP TIME: 20 MINUTES | COOK TIME: 20 MINUTES

Pressure-cooked chicken Marsala is savory, simple supper perfection. Mushrooms, onions, and spiced chicken cook—fast!—in a delicious mix of Marsala wine and chicken stock until juicy and tender. It is flavorful enough to serve when hosting guests for a meal, but it's simple enough to enjoy as a weeknight dinner, too.

½ cup all-purpose flour

1 teaspoon salt

½ teaspoon garlic powder

¼ teaspoon freshly ground black pepper

1 pound boneless, skinless chicken breasts (4 large pieces), pounded thin

2 tablespoons olive oil, divided

1 small onion, diced

6 ounces mushrooms, sliced

1 cup Marsala wine

½ cup chicken stock

Per serving: Calories: 307;
Total fat: 9g; Total carbs: 17g;
Fiber: 1g; Sugar: 2g; Protein: 30g;
Sodium: 748mg

1. In a large, shallow bowl, mix together the flour, salt, garlic powder, and pepper.

2. Dredge both sides of each chicken piece in the flour, shaking to remove any excess.

3. On an Instant Pot®, select Sauté and heat 1 tablespoon of olive oil. Cook the chicken in batches until it is slightly browned on both sides; remove from the pot and set aside.

4. Add the remaining 1 tablespoon of olive oil to the pot and cook the onion and mushrooms until slightly browned; press Cancel.

5. Add the Marsala wine and stock to the pot, followed by the chicken pieces.

6. Close and seal the Instant Pot, then select the Poultry setting and cook for 10 minutes.

7. Once cooking is finished, allow the pressure to release naturally for 5 minutes. Then manually release the remaining pressure and carefully open the pot.

Variation Tip: Prepare this dish on the stovetop in a large skillet: Cook the mushrooms and onions first, then add the chicken. When the chicken is cooked through, add the Marsala wine and stock. Cook until the sauce thickens slightly.

Instant Pot® Chicken Tortilla Soup

MEAT GLUTEN FREE GF GRAIN FREE NUT FREE SF SUGAR FREE

SERVES 4 TO 5 | PREP TIME: 5 MINUTES | COOK TIME: 15 MINUTES

This recipe is the one that made me fall in love with my Instant Pot. I was highly skeptical at first, but I decided to test drive it one night during dinner rush hour to see if it lived up to the hype. I threw some diced tomatoes, an onion, and some chicken in the pot, along with chicken stock and some spices, and I set it on High for 15 minutes. While it cooked, I made sure there was frozen pizza on hand to heat up just in case dinner didn't go as planned! Turns out I had no reason to fear—an Instant Pot is a lazy cook's (and busy mom's!) best friend. With minimal prep I was able to cook a fresh, savory chicken tortilla soup (without the tortillas!), and it's still a go-to supper.

3 large tomatoes, diced

1 onion, diced

1 pound boneless, skinless chicken breast (4 pieces)

1 teaspoon salt

1 teaspoon ground cumin

½ teaspoon ground coriander

4 cups chicken stock

Diced avocado, chopped fresh cilantro, and *Cilantro-Lime Sauce (page 134),* for topping (optional)

1. In an Instant Pot, combine the tomatoes, onion, and chicken. Season with the salt, cumin, and coriander, and pour in the chicken stock. Stir well.

2. Close and seal the Instant Pot, then select the Manual setting on high pressure for 15 minutes.

3. When cooking is finished, allow the pressure to release naturally.

4. Remove the chicken from the pot, shred it with two forks, and stir it back into the soup.

5. Serve with diced avocado, chopped cilantro, and Cilantro-Lime Sauce drizzled on top (if using). To add something crunchy, serve tortilla chips alongside.

Variation Tip: Add one (15-ounce) can of corn (drained and rinsed) and one can of black beans (drained and rinsed) to the pot before cooking for a heartier, thicker soup.

Per serving: Calories: 197; Total fat: 5g; Total carbs: 7g; Fiber: 2g; Sugar: 4g; Protein: 30g; Sodium: 1109mg

Rice with Edamame

P PAREVE G GLUTEN FREE NUT FREE SF SUGAR FREE V VEGAN

SERVES 8 TO 10 | PREP TIME: 5 MINUTES | COOK TIME: 5 MINUTES

Rice with edamame is a delicious side that cooks up super soft and fluffy in an Instant Pot®. This dish is a total little-kid favorite, since it has a mostly neutral flavor with just a bit of texture from the edamame. You can also swap out the edamame for broccoli or shredded carrots if you like.

1 onion, diced

2 cups white basmati rice

2 cups vegetable stock

12 ounces frozen edamame

1 teaspoon salt

1. In an Instant Pot, combine the onion, rice, vegetable stock, edamame, and salt.

2. Close and seal the Instant Pot, then select the Manual setting on high pressure and cook for 3 minutes.

3. Once the cooking is finished, allow the pressure to release naturally.

4. Fluff the rice with a fork before serving.

Per serving: Calories: 262; Total fat: 3g; Total carbs: 47g; Fiber: 5g; Sugar: 1g; Protein: 13g; Sodium: 485mg

Slow Cooker Poached Pears

P PAREVE **G** GLUTEN FREE **GF** GRAIN FREE **◎** NUT FREE **V** VEGAN

SERVES 6 TO 8 | PREP TIME: 10 MINUTES | COOK TIME: 4 TO 6 HOURS

I picked up this recipe one weekend at my sister Tova's house. When I first started cooking, she was my guide, always sharing her secrets to the quick dinners that her family would actually eat. (She has seven children, so I find that quite impressive!) She is known for her sweets, like chocolate chip cookies, cupcakes, and this grown-up favorite. I love how the pears soak up the sweet wine and end up tasting like an adult version of the sweet, syrupy fruit cocktails I enjoyed as a child.

1¼ cups sweet red wine

3 cups water

½ cup sugar

1 tablespoon vanilla extract

1 teaspoon ground cinnamon

6 to 8 pears, peeled

1. In a slow cooker, combine the red wine, water, sugar, vanilla extract, and cinnamon.
2. Add the pears, laying them on their sides and ensuring they are submerged in the wine mixture. Cover and cook on Low for 4 to 6 hours or until pears are tender when pierced with a fork.

Variation Tip: This can also be cooked on the stovetop. Place all the ingredients except for the pears in a large pot. Bring to a boil, then place the pears in the pot and simmer for 45 minutes.

Ingredient Tip: The best pears for poaching are Bosc, Anjou, or Bartlett varieties. An optional trick: cut a small slice from the bottom of each pear before poaching. This way, they'll stand up nicely when serving.

Per serving: Calories: 232; Total fat: 0g; Total carbs: 50g; Fiber: 7g; Sugar: 38g; Protein: 1g; Sodium: 6mg

Chapter Seven

BAKERY

Chocolate Chip Zucchini Walnut Muffins

 PAREVE VEGETARIAN

MAKES 12 MUFFINS | PREP TIME: 5 MINUTES | COOK TIME: 25 MINUTES

These muffins are moist and soft, with a rich cinnamon flavor that almost makes you forget that there is actual zucchini in the batter. My toddler is crazy about them—he calls them "mommy muffins"—I'd like to think it's because I'm the one making them, but it's more likely due to the fact that I am always stealing bites from his!

Nonstick cooking spray

1 cup sugar

1 cup canola oil

3 eggs

1 tablespoon vanilla extract

2 cups all-purpose flour

2 teaspoons baking soda

2 teaspoons ground cinnamon

1 teaspoon salt

¼ teaspoon baking powder

2 cups grated zucchini (from 2 medium zucchini, no need to peel)

1 cup semisweet vegan chocolate chips

¾ cup chopped walnuts

1. Preheat the oven to 350°F. Grease a 12-cup muffin pan with nonstick cooking spray or line the cups with cupcake liners.

2. In a large bowl, whisk together the sugar, oil, eggs, and vanilla. Add the flour, baking soda, cinnamon, salt, and baking powder and mix well. Fold in the shredded zucchini, then fold in the chocolate chips.

3. Scoop the batter into the prepared muffin pan. Top each cup with chopped walnuts.

4. Bake for about 24 minutes or until the tops of the muffins are slightly browned and a toothpick inserted in the center comes out clean.

Make-ahead Tip: These muffins freeze well, so you can bake a batch in advance and keep your freezer stocked for when you need a good dessert on demand.

Variation Tip: This recipe can also be baked in a loaf pan or Bundt pan. If using a loaf pan, bake for 50 minutes in two greased 10-inch loaf pans, or bake in one Bundt pan for about an hour.

Per serving (1 muffin): Calories: 479; Total fat: 31g; Total carbs: 39g; Fiber: 3g; Sugar: 29g; Protein: 6g; Sodium: 424mg

Cranberry Apple Puff Pastry Cups

P PAREVE **I** DAIRY **V** VEGETARIAN

MAKES 40 CUPS | PREP TIME: 15 MINUTES | COOK TIME: 25 MINUTES

The flavors (and volume!) of this quick and easy dessert make it perfect for Thanksgiving, but this dessert also works as an addition to any holiday menu. Top the cups with the cinnamon glaze, a scoop of ice cream, or whipped cream for an even more decadent treat.

FOR THE CUPS

Nonstick cooking spray

3 Gala apples, peeled and diced

8 ounces cranberries

½ cup all-purpose flour

½ cup sugar

1 stick (½ cup) margarine

1 teaspoon ground cinnamon

10 (5-inch) puff pastry squares

FOR THE CINNAMON GLAZE

¾ cup powdered sugar

1 tablespoon almond milk

1 teaspoon vanilla extract

⅛ teaspoon ground cinnamon

TO MAKE THE CUPS

1. Preheat the oven to 375°F. Grease two 24-cup mini muffin pans with nonstick cooking spray.

2. In a large mixing bowl, combine the apples and cranberries.

3. In a separate large mixing bowl, combine the flour, sugar, margarine, and cinnamon. Using your hands, work the ingredients together until they are the crumbly texture of a crumb topping.

4. Cut each puff pastry square into 4 mini squares, and press each mini square into a cup in your prepared mini muffin pan. Fill each pastry cup with some of the cranberry-apple mixture and top with the crumb topping mixture.

5. Bake for 25 to 30 minutes or until the pastry is puffed and slightly browned.

TO MAKE THE CINNAMON GLAZE

1. In a small bowl, whisk together the powdered sugar, almond milk, vanilla, and cinnamon until smooth.

2. Top the pastry cups with the glaze before serving.

Per serving (2 pastry cups): Calories: 198; Total fat: 11g; Total carbs: 24g; Fiber: 1g; Sugar: 13g; Protein: 2g; Sodium: 116mg

Vegan Toaster Pastries

 PAREVE ♥ **FAMILY FAVORITE** ⓥ **VEGAN**

MAKES ABOUT 6 PASTRIES | PREP TIME: 20 MINUTES | COOK TIME: 25 MINUTES

There is nothing like frosted, sprinkled toaster pastries to bring out your inner child. This version of everyone's favorite childhood snack is vegan but still has the classic elements of soft cookies stuffed with strawberry jam. I wanted to create this recipe using a vegan dough so I could bake them with my toddler and not have to worry about him sneaking a few bites of the uncooked dough. Although, if I'm being honest, it's kind of my favorite thing to do, too!

FOR THE PASTRIES

2 tablespoons ground flaxseed combined with 6 tablespoons water

⅔ cup sugar

½ cup oil

1 teaspoon vanilla extract

2½ cups all-purpose flour

2 teaspoons baking powder

1 cup raspberry jam

1 cup sprinkles, for decorating

FOR THE ICING

¾ cup powdered sugar

1 tablespoon almond milk

1 teaspoon vanilla extract

TO MAKE THE PASTRIES

1. Preheat the oven to 350°F.
2. Using an electric mixer, combine the flaxseed mixture, sugar, oil, and vanilla.
3. Slowly add the flour and baking powder to the mixer and combine. The dough might be crumbly; remove the bowl from the mixer and use your hands to smooth and incorporate all the ingredients.
4. Roll the dough out onto a floured surface and cut out 12 palm-size rectangles.
5. Dollop 1 tablespoon of jam into the center of half of the dough rectangles, then cover each with a separate rectangle of dough, gently pressing the edges down. Using a fork, crimp the edges all around.
6. Prepare a baking sheet lined with parchment paper. Place the pastries on the baking sheet and bake for 20 to 25 minutes. Set aside to cool.

TO MAKE THE ICING

1. Combine the powdered sugar, almond milk, and vanilla until smooth.

2. Once the pastries are cool, frost the top of each pastry and add sprinkles before the icing hardens.

. . . .

Variation Tip: Instead of rectangles, use a cookie cutter to create fun shapes such as hearts, triangles, or circles. You can also cut out smaller shapes and insert a stick in between the layers of dough to bake them on a stick.

. . . .

Per serving: Calories: 607; Total fat: 21g; Total carbs: 103g; Fiber: 2g; Sugar: 58g; Protein: 5g; Sodium: 3mg

Strawberry Crumb Cupcakes

 PAREVE NUT FREE  VEGAN

MAKES 20 CUPCAKES | PREP TIME: 5 MINUTES | COOK TIME: 25 MINUTES

These cupcakes are light and fluffy with a delicate crumb topping and a surprise filling of freshly chopped strawberries. Whether you are baking a batch for a new neighbor, serving them to friends for a birthday celebration, or baking them as a weekend treat to enjoy on Shabbat, each bite will bring little bits of joy.

3 cups all-purpose flour, divided

1⅓ cups granulated sugar

3 teaspoons baking powder

1 teaspoon salt

½ cup oil

1 cup orange juice

2 eggs

2 teaspoons vanilla extract, divided

1 cup chopped strawberries

1 cup light brown sugar

1 stick (½ cup) margarine, cubed

¾ cup powdered sugar

1 tablespoon almond milk

1. Preheat the oven to 350°F. Line a 12-cup muffin pan with paper liners or spray the cups with nonstick cooking spray.

2. In a large mixing bowl, mix together 2 cups of flour, the granulated sugar, baking powder, salt, oil, orange juice, eggs, and 1 teaspoon of vanilla. Fold in the chopped strawberries.

3. Using an ice cream scoop, fill the prepared muffin cups three-quarters full.

4. In another mixing bowl, make the topping by combining the remaining 1 cup of flour, the brown sugar, and margarine. Using your hands, mix until it resembles wet sand.

5. Top each cup of batter with 1 tablespoon of topping.

6. Bake for 22 to 24 minutes or until a toothpick inserted into the center of a cupcake comes out clean.

7. Meanwhile, make the icing: In a small bowl, whisk together the powdered sugar, almond milk, and remaining 1 teaspoon of vanilla.

8. Let the cupcakes cool completely, then drizzle the icing over the top.

Variation Tip: Instead of making cupcakes, bake the batter in a 9-by-13-inch baking dish for a delicious strawberry crumb cake. Extend the baking time to about 40 minutes total, or until a toothpick inserted in the center comes out clean.

Per serving: Calories: 358; Total fat: 14g; Total carbs: 56g; Fiber: 1g; Sugar: 35g; Protein: 4g; Sodium: 239mg

Lemon Blueberry Cake with Buttercream Frosting

 **P** PAREVE **⊗** NUT FREE **V** VEGETARIAN

MAKES ONE 9-BY-13-INCH CAKE (SERVES 16) | PREP TIME: 5 MINUTES | COOK TIME: 45 MINUTES

To say my mom is a baker is an understatement. She is the queen of cakes, danishes, donuts, and all things sweet. Thanks to her, I always like to have something freshly baked on the kitchen counter. This lemon blueberry cake is one of my favorites.

FOR THE CAKE

2 cups all-purpose flour

1⅓ cups sugar

3 teaspoons
baking powder

1 teaspoon salt

½ cup oil

1 cup soy milk (original,
unflavored)

2 eggs

1 teaspoon vanilla extract

½ teaspoon lemon extract

Zest of 2 lemons

1 cup blueberries

FOR THE BUTTERCREAM FROSTING

1 (16-ounce) box
powdered sugar

¼ cup soy milk (original,
unflavored)

1 teaspoon vanilla extract

1 stick (½ cup) margarine,
at room temperature

TO MAKE THE CAKE

1. Preheat the oven to 350°F. Line a 9-by-13-inch baking dish with parchment paper.

2. In a large mixing bowl, combine the flour, sugar, baking powder, salt, oil, soy milk, eggs, vanilla, lemon extract, and lemon zest. Add the blueberries to the batter and combine.

3. Spread the batter in the prepared baking dish and bake for 40 to 45 minutes or until a toothpick inserted comes out clean. Allow the cake to cool before frosting with the buttercream.

TO MAKE THE BUTTERCREAM FROSTING

In a large mixing bowl, using an electric mixer, cream together the powdered sugar, soy milk, vanilla, and margarine until smooth.

Variation Tip: Omit the blueberries and lemon zest and stir in 1 cup rainbow sprinkles for a deliciously fun confetti cake perfect for birthday celebrations.

Per serving: Calories: 366; Total fat: 14g; Total carbs: 60g; Fiber: 1g; Sugar: 46g; Protein: 3g; Sodium: 233mg

Classic Creamy Cheesecake

 DAIRY NUT FREE VEGETARIAN

MAKES ONE 9-INCH CHEESECAKE (SERVES 8) | PREP TIME: 10 MINUTES | COOK TIME: 1 HOUR

You can keep this cheesecake classic or serve it with a variety of different toppings. I have tested out many cheesecake recipes, but I always find myself coming back to this one for both the flavor and the memories. I got the recipe from my best friend Henny's mom. Her name was Bella, and she was an amazing baker. I would spend many Shabbat mornings with them, laughing over slices of cheesecake and chocolate cake with sour cream. This recipe is a reminder to savor life, one bite at a time.

12 ounces whipped cream cheese (1½ 8-ounce packages), at room temperature

½ cup sour cream

2 eggs

½ cup sugar

1 tablespoon vanilla sugar or vanilla extract

1 (9-inch) prepared graham cracker crust, from the baking section

1. Preheat the oven to 350°F.
2. In a large mixing bowl, using an electric mixer, beat the cream cheese, sour cream, eggs, sugar, and vanilla together.
3. Pour the mixture into the graham cracker crust.
4. Bake for 45 minutes to an hour, until the top of the cheesecake is set.

Variation Tip: The topping possibilities are endless when it comes to cheesecake: try whipped cream and your favorite cereal, such as Fruity Pebbles or Reese's Puffs. Or drizzle melted chocolate and top with chopped candy bars (to quickly melt chocolate, place 1 cup chocolate chips in a microwave-safe dish and melt in 30-second increments; add 1 teaspoon canola oil once melted for a smoother texture). To make a s'mores cheesecake, top with mini marshmallows and chocolate chips and, once baked, sprinkle crushed graham cracker crumbs on top.

Per serving: Calories: 310; Total fat: 19g; Total carbs: 31g; Fiber: 0g; Sugar: 23g; Protein: 5g; Sodium: 321mg

Chocolate Cinnamon Bread Pudding

P PAREVE   **♡** FAMILY FAVORITE   **⊗** NUT FREE   **V** VEGETARIAN

SERVES 5 TO 7 | PREP TIME: 10 MINUTES | COOK TIME: 30 MINUTES

Bread pudding is one of those indulgent recipes that I always assumed must be complicated to make—but it's actually really easy. A basic bread pudding starts off with a good sturdy egg bread, such as challah, brioche, or French bread, cut into chunks. Once baked, the final dish has slightly crispy edges with a custardlike center. It's delicious as is and even more decadent served with ice cream or whipped cream and some fresh raspberries or blueberries.

1 large loaf Challah (page 122), torn into bite-size pieces

1 cup broken-up dark chocolate pieces

2 cups soy milk

2 eggs

1 teaspoon vanilla extract

1 teaspoon ground cinnamon

¼ cup brown sugar

1. Preheat the oven to 350°F. Line a 9-by-13-inch baking pan with parchment paper.

2. Place the pieces of challah in the baking pan. Place the chocolate pieces in between the pieces of challah.

3. In a large bowl, whisk together the soy milk, eggs, vanilla, cinnamon, and brown sugar.

4. Pour the milk mixture over the challah and chocolate. Press the challah down in the pan so every piece of challah gets coated in the milk mixture.

5. Bake for about 30 minutes or until the edges are slightly crispy and the chocolate has melted.

Variation Tip: Make this a dairy dish by swapping out the soy milk for heavy cream and adding chunks of milk chocolate. Serve warm with powdered sugar, ice cream, whipped cream, or fresh fruit.

Per serving: Calories: 419; Total fat: 14g; Total carbs: 66g; Fiber: 12g; Sugar: 24g; Protein: 13g; Sodium: 396mg

Apple Pie Egg Rolls

 PAREVE   NUT FREE   **V** VEGAN

MAKES 8 TO 10 EGG ROLLS | PREP TIME: 10 MINUTES | COOK TIME: 35 MINUTES

I love giving the familiar flavors I love an exciting new twist. My mom always baked the most delicious apple pie for Rosh Hashanah during the fall season. The kitchen would be filled with the sweet smell of apples and cinnamon, letting us know a feast was being prepared. This recipe keeps the apple pie filling, baked to perfection in egg roll wrappers for individual-size portions. They make for a traditional yet novel holiday treat.

¼ cup packed
brown sugar

2 teaspoons ground
cinnamon

¼ teaspoon allspice
(or nutmeg)

2 tablespoons
all-purpose flour

2 large apples (Gala or
Granny Smith), peeled,
cored, and diced

Juice of 1 lemon

8 to 10 egg roll wrappers

Canola oil, for frying

¼ cup powdered sugar,
for serving

*Cinnamon Coconut
Whipped Cream
(page 27),* for serving

1. In a medium mixing bowl, combine the brown sugar, cinnamon, allspice, and flour.

2. In a large bowl, combine the diced apples with the lemon juice. Add the brown sugar mixture and mix well.

3. Place 1 to 2 tablespoons of apples in the center of each egg roll wrapper, then wet the edges and roll up.

4. Line a plate with paper towels. Coat a large skillet with oil and place it over high heat. When the oil is hot, add the egg rolls and fry them until golden brown on all sides.

5. Place the fried egg rolls on the paper towel–lined plate to soak up excess oil, then dust them with powdered sugar. Serve with Coconut Cinnamon Whipped Cream.

Variation Tip: Instead of frying, you can bake the egg rolls in a 375°F oven for about 15 to 20 minutes until golden brown.

Per serving: Calories: 218; Total fat: 4g; Total carbs: 41g; Fiber: 3g; Sugar: 14g; Protein: 4g; Sodium: 232mg

Strawberry Cheese Danish

DAIRY **NUT FREE** **V VEGETARIAN**

MAKES 2 LARGE DANISH PASTRIES (SERVES 8) | PREP TIME: 10 MINUTES | COOK TIME: 25 MINUTES

I always have at least one or two packages of puff pastry in my freezer, just waiting to be baked into something delicious. It's a great item to have on hand when you are short on time and want to bake a quick dessert. It can be filled, stuffed, or rolled with a variety of things, and one of my favorite combos is this sweet cream cheese and strawberry jam.

1 (17.3-ounce) package frozen puff pastry sheets (two sheets), thawed

1 (8-ounce) package cream cheese, at room temperature, divided

⅓ cup granulated sugar

2 teaspoons vanilla extract, divided

1 cup strawberry jam, divided

¾ cup powdered sugar

1 tablespoon milk

1. Preheat the oven to 350°F. Line a baking sheet with parchment paper.

2. Using a rolling pin, roll both sheets of puff pastry out until flattened.

3. In a large mixing bowl, combine the cream cheese, sugar, and 1 teaspoon of vanilla.

4. Place half of the cream cheese mixture in the center of one sheet of rolled puff pastry, spreading it down the middle without reaching the edges. Spread ½ cup of strawberry jam on top of the cream cheese.

5. Cut slits into the dough on either side of the cheese mixture. Starting from one end, crisscross the strands of dough over the cheese filling, creating a braid. Repeat the process with the remaining sheet of puff pastry. Transfer the pastries to the prepared baking sheet.

6. Bake for 20 to 25 minutes or until the pastry is puffed up and slightly golden.

7. Meanwhile, make the icing: In a small bowl, whisk together the powdered sugar, milk, and remaining 1 teaspoon of vanilla until smooth.

8. Allow the pastries to cool before drizzling them with the icing.

Variation Tip: Try chocolate hazelnut spread instead of jam, or break a chocolate bar into large pieces and place directly on top of the cream cheese mixture before baking.

Per serving: Calories: 570; Total fat: 25g; Total carbs: 82g; Fiber: 2g; Sugar: 22g; Protein: 7g; Sodium: 295mg

Classic Challah with Modern Variations

P PAREVE NUT FREE | MAKES 4 LARGE LOAVES (SERVES 32)
PREP TIME: 30 MINUTES ACTIVE, 3 HOURS INACTIVE | COOK TIME: 40 MINUTES

This classic challah recipe is slightly sweet with a soft, cakelike texture. It is my bubbe's recipe, and it is a constant on my Shabbat table. While baking challah can be somewhat of a tedious process (kneading the dough and then waiting for it to rise before shaping), the end result—slices of challah hot from the oven topped with fresh hummus—is always worth it.

3 (¼-ounce) packets active dry yeast

3½ cups warm water (about 100°F), divided

2 teaspoons sugar

1 cup canola oil

1¾ cups sugar

1 tablespoon salt

1 teaspoon vanilla extract

6 eggs, divided

12 cups all-purpose flour

1 tablespoon water

1. Preheat the oven to 300°F. Line a baking sheet with parchment paper.

2. In a medium bowl, combine the yeast with ½ cup of warm water and the sugar and let it sit until it begins to bubble, 5 to 10 minutes.

3. Meanwhile, in a large bowl, combine the remaining 3 cups warm water, oil, sugar, salt, vanilla, and 4 eggs, and mix well. Then add the yeast mixture and mix well. Add the flour and stir to combine, mixing until all of the flour is incorporated.

4. Cover the bowl with a clean kitchen towel and let the dough rise for 3 to 4 hours, until it has puffed up and about doubled in volume.

5. Divide the dough into 4 equal pieces. If the dough is sticky, dust your surface with flour. Divide each piece of dough into three sections, roll the sections into long ropes, and braid them, pinching the ends to seal. Place the braided loaves on the prepared baking sheet. Cover and allow to rise a second time, for about 40 minutes.

6. In a small bowl, whisk the remaining 2 eggs with 1 tablespoon of water. Brush the braided loaves with the egg wash.

7. Bake the loaves for 20 minutes, then increase the oven temperature to 350°F and bake for another 20 minutes or until the tops are golden brown.

Variation Tip: After brushing the tops of your loaves with egg yolk, you can top them with sesame seeds, everything-bagel spice, sugar-cinnamon mix, or other favorite spices. To make a stuffed challah, separate the prepared dough into small pieces as you shape it, then roll out each piece into long strands. Flatten the strands and place your filling along each. (Try s'mores challah with a schmear of chocolate spread down the center, plus mini marshmallows and chocolate chips.) Then seal each strand by rolling it over and pressing down the side before braiding. Brush braided challah with egg yolk mixture and add toppings (in this case, crushed graham crackers and additional chocolate chips and mini marshmallows). For a savory stuffing, stuff with chopped pastrami and barbecue sauce and top the braided challah with crispy onions before baking.

Per serving: Calories: 286; Total fat: 8g; Total carbs: 47g; Fiber: 2g; Sugar: 11g; Protein: 6g; Sodium: 230mg

Sweet Potato Pie

P PAREVE   NUT FREE   **V** VEGETARIAN

MAKES ONE 6-OUNCE PIE (SERVES 8) | PREP TIME: 15 MINUTES | COOK TIME: 2 HOURS

This pie is another winning recipe given to me by my big sister, Tova. (I wasn't joking when I said she was my guru of all things cooking and baking.) I remember there were many nights I would call her in a panic, new in the kitchen and having no idea what I was doing. She always had a solution with tons of quick and simple recipes. This sweet potato pie is one that has saved my dinner menu countless times—it never fails, it's easy to prep, and it's always delicious.

3 large sweet potatoes

3 eggs

¾ cup orange juice

¼ cup canola oil

1 teaspoon vanilla extract

1 teaspoon ground cinnamon

½ teaspoon salt

½ cup brown sugar

1 (9-inch) prepared graham cracker crust, from the baking section

1. Preheat the oven to 350°F.

2. Peel and halve the sweet potatoes. Place them in a large pot of water and bring the water to a boil. Cook the sweet potatoes until they are soft, 45 to 60 minutes.

3. Once cooked, drain the water and, using an immersion blender, mash the potatoes.

4. In a large mixing bowl, combine the eggs, orange juice, oil, vanilla, cinnamon, salt, and sugar. Add the mashed sweet potatoes and mix well.

5. Place the sweet potato mixture in the graham cracker crust and bake for 45 minutes to an hour, until the mixture is set and the edges are slightly browned.

Variation Tip: Cover the pie with mini marshmallows in the last 15 minutes of baking for a delicious topping.

Per serving: Calories: 278; Total fat: 14g; Total carbs: 35g; Fiber: 2g; Sugar: 21g; Protein: 4g; Sodium: 321mg

Chocolate Chip Banana Crumb Cake

 PAREVE  NUT FREE **V** VEGETARIAN

MAKES ONE 9-BY-13-INCH CAKE (SERVES 12) | PREP TIME: 5 MINUTES | COOK TIME: 35 MINUTES

There is something so comforting about a slice of banana cake. With a layer of crumb topping and chocolate chips studded throughout, it's the ultimate comfort cake. Whenever I buy bananas, I always make sure to keep two hidden away, just so I have an excuse to bake this dessert when I "forget" them and they begin to brown.

1½ sticks (¾ cup) margarine, at room temperature, plus 1 stick (½ cup) margarine, chilled, divided

1½ cups sugar

2 eggs

½ cup apple juice

3 cups all-purpose flour, divided

1 teaspoon baking soda

1 teaspoon baking powder

1 teaspoon vanilla extract

1 cup mashed banana (from 2 bananas)

1 cup light brown sugar

¼ teaspoon ground cinnamon

¼ cup semisweet vegan chocolate chips (optional)

1. Preheat the oven to 350°F. Line a 9-by-13-inch baking dish with parchment paper.

2. Using electric beaters, combine ¾ cup of margarine, the sugar, and eggs. Add the apple juice, 2 cups of flour, the baking soda, baking powder, and vanilla and mix well. Add in the mashed bananas and combine. Scrape the batter into the prepared baking dish.

3. In a medium mixing bowl, make the topping by combining the remaining 1 cup of flour, the brown sugar, the remaining ½ cup of margarine, and the cinnamon, using your hands to create a crumb texture. Top the cake with the crumb topping and sprinkle with the chocolate chips (if using).

4. Bake for 35 minutes or until the cake is set.

Variation Tip: Skip the chocolate chips and crumb topping and bake the batter in two greased 10-inch loaf pans for 50 minutes for a more traditional banana bread.

Per serving: Calories: 389; Total fat: 13g; Total carbs: 67g; Fiber: 1g; Sugar: 40g; Protein: 5g; Sodium: 252mg

Funfetti® Hamantaschen

P PAREVE   ♥ FAMILY FAVORITE   ⊗ NUT FREE   **V** VEGETARIAN

MAKES 20 COOKIES | PREP TIME: 15 MINUTES | COOK TIME: 15 MINUTES

We celebrate the Jewish holiday Purim by dressing up in costume, giving out candy, and eating a triangle-shaped pastry called hamantaschen. This pastry has a cookielike texture and is traditionally stuffed with apricot, raspberry, and prune filling. However, I enjoy using nontraditional ingredients to give the standard dish a fun and festive makeover. After all, this holiday is all about joy.

⅔ cup sugar

½ cup oil

2 eggs

1 teaspoon vanilla extract

2½ cups all-purpose flour

2 teaspoons baking powder

½ cup rainbow sprinkles

1 cup strawberry or raspberry jam

1. Preheat the oven to 350°F. Line a baking sheet with parchment paper.

2. In a large mixing bowl using electric beaters, cream together the sugar, oil, eggs, and vanilla. Slowly add in the flour and baking powder and mix well. The dough might be crumbly, so feel free to put aside the beaters and use your hands.

3. Add the sprinkles slowly, depending on how many you want in the dough; don't overmix or crush them.

4. Roll the dough out onto a floured surface to about ¼- to ⅛-inch thickness. (If too thick, the dough will be difficult to shape and won't stick together. If too thin, it may rip when shaping or filling.) Cut out circles using a large circle cookie cutter or the rim of a large glass or mason jar.

5. Fill the center of the circle of dough with 1 teaspoon of jam.

6. Fold the sides of the dough over, pinching the corners to create a triangle shape. (To shape hamantaschen like an expert, slowly fold over one side. Then fold the next side, and finally fold the bottom up. Gently pinch the corners. You can also simply bring up the sides, forming a triangle by pinching the corners together.)

7. Bake the hamantaschen for 12 to 15 minutes, depending on how soft or crispy you want them. I like them super soft so I usually remove from the oven after 12 minutes.

....

Variation Tip: You can drizzle melted chocolate over the baked hamantaschen and top with more sprinkles. You can swap jam filling for chocolate filling. Or, you can make lemon bar–flavored hamantaschen by stuffing the cookies with lemon pudding and then dusting them with powdered sugar when they come out of the oven.

....

Per serving (1 cookie): Calories: 222; Total fat: 7g; Total carbs: 37g; Fiber: 0g; Sugar: 10g; Protein: 2g; Sodium: 7mg

Hamantaschen Ice Cream Sandwiches

DAIRY ♥ **FAMILY FAVORITE** ⊘ **NUT FREE** Ⓥ **VEGETARIAN**

MAKES 10 SANDWICHES | PREP TIME: 10 MINUTES

Hamantaschen ice cream sandwiches are the ultimate Purim treat! Create a hamantaschen ice cream sandwich bar with the crispy triangle-shaped cookies, an assortment of ice cream flavors, and toppings such as sprinkles, crushed cookies, chopped chocolate bars, and melted chocolate—then let everyone have fun creating their favorite combinations.

20 Hamantaschen cookies (page 126), cooled to room temperature if just baked

1 cup chocolate chips

½ cup sprinkles

Crushed cookies, chopped chocolate bars, and favorite cereals, for topping (optional)

2½ cups ice cream (any flavor)

1. While waiting for the hamantaschen to cool, heat the chocolate chips in the microwave in 30-second increments, stirring at intervals until melted.

2. Drizzle the melted chocolate over the cooled cookies, then immediately top half of the cookies with sprinkles and other toppings of your choice.

3. Allow the chocolate drizzle to dry completely, then add a scoop of ice cream to each decorated cookie and top with another chocolate-drizzled hamantaschen. (Alternately, you can just sandwich two cookies with ice cream and then drizzle with the melted chocolate and garnish with toppings.)

Variation Tip: Create a hamantaschen ice cream bar by setting up bowls of different flavors of ice cream, melted chocolate, and fun toppings and letting everyone create and decorate their own ice cream sandwiches.

Per serving (1 sandwich): Calories: 568; Total fat: 21g; Total carbs: 88g; Fiber: 1g; Sugar: 32g; Protein: 6g; Sodium: 41mg

Brownie Truffles

P PAREVE

MAKES 12 TO 15 TRUFFLES | PREP TIME: 5 MINUTES | COOK TIME: 25 MINUTES

The lazy hostess in me thinks it is imperative that everyone has at least one ridiculously easy, "semi-homemade" dessert recipe that is also impressively delicious. This would be that recipe. Here, chocolate fudge brownies (from a box!) are rolled into bite-size confections and dusted with an assortment of toppings (such as cocoa powder, powdered sugar, colorful sprinkles, and coarse sea salt), creating a display of decadent desserts that are as simple to make as they are delicious to eat.

1 box dairy-free brownie mix

⅓ cup water

⅓ cup oil

1 egg

12 ounces bittersweet or semisweet chocolate

Sprinkles, cocoa powder, sea salt, or melted white chocolate, for topping (optional)

1. Preheat the oven to 350°F. Prepare a 9-by-13-inch baking dish.

2. In a large mixing bowl, stir together the brownie mix, water, oil, and egg.

3. Pour the batter into the baking dish and spread it out evenly. Bake for 20 to 25 minutes. The edges should be slightly crispy but the center should still be soft. Remove from the oven and let cool completely.

4. Invert the cake onto a cutting board and cut off the edges if they are crispy. Using a fork, mash the entire brownie. Scoop out ½ tablespoon of brownie and shape it into a ball. Do this until you have used all the mashed brownie.

5. Melt the chocolate in a microwave-safe bowl in 30-second increments, stirring after each. Using a spoon, drizzle the melted chocolate over the brownie balls. Press the toppings of your choice into the truffles before the chocolate hardens.

6. Serve the brownie truffles in mini cupcake papers.

Per serving: Calories: 308; Total fat: 14g; Total carbs: 42g; Fiber: 5g; Sugar: 30g; Protein: 3g; Sodium: 124mg

Gluten-Free Brownie S'mores

P PAREVE **♥** FAMILY FAVORITE **G** GLUTEN FREE **⊗** NUT FREE **V** VEGETARIAN

MAKES ONE 9-BY-13-INCH PAN (SERVES 12) | PREP TIME: 5 MINUTES | COOK TIME: 25 MINUTES

My mom makes the best tray of brownies on the block. Her chocolate fudge, gluten-free brownie s'mores are the reason I don't dread Passover and its lack of gluten desserts. This is a family favorite and always made our home the place to be. Be prepared to make a double batch of this recipe, since it's usually devoured within minutes of leaving the oven. This recipe is perfect for Passover and year-round whenever you need a delicious gluten-free dessert.

½ cup oil

4 eggs

1½ cups sugar

½ cup potato starch

½ cup cocoa powder

1 cup mini or regular marshmallows

1 cup vegan chocolate chips

1. Preheat the oven to 350°F. Prepare a 9-by-13-inch baking dish.

2. In a large mixing bowl, combine the oil, eggs, sugar, potato starch, and cocoa powder. Pour the batter into the baking dish and spread it out evenly.

3. Bake for about 20 minutes, then layer the marshmallows and chocolate chips on top and continue baking for an additional 5 minutes or until the marshmallows have browned and the chocolate chips have melted.

Variation Tip: Make cheesecake brownies by spreading the brownie batter in the baking pan, then topping it with raw cheesecake batter (see page 117). Bake at 350°F for about 35 minutes or until the cheesecake layer is slightly browned on top.

Per serving: Calories: 348; Total fat: 19g; Total carbs: 48g; Fiber: 2g; Sugar: 36g; Protein: 4g; Sodium: 25mg

Strawberry Apple Crumble

 DAIRY   NUT FREE

MAKES 1 PIE | PREP TIME: 5 MINUTES | COOK TIME: 30 MINUTES

This sweet strawberry apple crumble (baked in a deep-dish piecrust) has become my signature dessert. My sister Mushky knows to expect it whenever she comes over to eat. In fact, the few times I have swapped it for a different dessert, she was disappointed—and I was reminded not to mess with the classics. Use any combination of fruit that you have in your refrigerator (or freezer!)—it's a great way to use up leftover fruit that might otherwise go bad. If you do not have a piecrust on hand, this can also be served in a baking dish using the crumble topping as a crust, or simply skip that step and it can be baked as a strawberry apple brown betty.

12 strawberries, halved or quartered

2 Gala apples, peeled and cubed

1 deep-dish piecrust, from the freezer section

1 teaspoon freshly squeezed lemon juice

½ cup all-purpose flour

½ cup sugar

½ teaspoon ground cinnamon

½ stick (¼ cup) margarine or Earth Balance

1. Preheat the oven to 350°F.
2. Place the strawberries and apples in the piecrust and drizzle with the lemon juice.
3. In a large mixing bowl, combine the flour, sugar, cinnamon, and margarine. Using your hands, mix until the mixture looks like wet sand.
4. Scrape the crumble mixture over the fruit in the piecrust and spread it evenly.
5. Bake for about 30 minutes or until the crust is slightly browned.

Variation Tip: You can use any fruit combo you like! I often make this using strawberries and peaches, a combo of berries, or just apples. Serve it warm with ice cream, but it also tastes great cold or at room temperature.

Per serving: Calories: 225; Total fat: 11g; Total carbs: 30g; Fiber: 1g; Sugar: 17g; Protein: 2g; Sodium: 169mg

QUICK STIR-FRY MARINADE *page 135*

Chapter Eight
STAPLES

Cilantro-Lime Sauce

P PAREVE **G** GLUTEN FREE **GF** GRAIN FREE **⊘** NUT FREE **SF** SUGAR FREE **V** VEGETARIAN

MAKES ABOUT ½ CUP | PREP TIME: 5 MINUTES

I like this cilantro-lime dipping sauce so much that I often plan my dinner menu based entirely on whether or not I can pair it with this sauce. Turns out, there really isn't any dish that doesn't taste better with this drizzled on top of it. I like to layer it over my spiced baked salmon or roasted veggies, serve it on kani bites, and dip my crispy tofu sticks in it. Freshly chopped cilantro and lime juice are a winning flavor combo in my book.

½ cup mayonnaise

2 tablespoons chopped fresh cilantro

Juice of ½ lime

¼ teaspoon chili powder

In a medium bowl, whisk together the mayonnaise, cilantro, lime juice, and chili powder until well blended and smooth.

Per serving (2 tablespoons): Calories: 183; Total fat: 20g; Total carbs: 1g; Fiber: 0g; Sugar: 0g; Protein: 0g; Sodium: 180mg

Quick Stir-Fry Marinade

P PAREVE **GF** GRAIN FREE **⊗** NUT FREE **V** VEGETARIAN

MAKES ABOUT ½ CUP | PREP TIME: 5 MINUTES

I love Chinese food for dinner, but not the price and grease that come with it. So, I created this sweet and salty marinade for cooking takeout-inspired chicken, tofu, beef, or veggies at home. Simply cook your protein or veggies in a large skillet or wok, add this sauce, and stir until thickened.

¼ cup honey

¼ cup soy sauce

¼ cup water

1 tablespoon cornstarch

In a medium bowl, whisk together the honey, soy sauce, water, and cornstarch.

Variation Tip: Add crushed garlic and grated fresh ginger to the sauce for enhanced flavor.

Per serving (2 tablespoons): Calories: 80; Total fat: 0g; Total carbs: 19g; Fiber: 0g; Sugar: 18g; Protein: 1g; Sodium: 900mg

Sweet Tahini Dressing

P PAREVE **G** GLUTEN FREE **GF** GRAIN FREE **V** VEGETARIAN

MAKES ABOUT ½ CUP | PREP TIME: 5 MINUTES

The first time I used tahini as a dressing over my salad, I was amazed at how creamy it was and loved the texture it brought to my kale and avocado bowl. Since then, I have drizzled it over roasted butternut squash, baked potatoes stuffed with sausage and peppers, slices of grilled chicken, cubed tofu, and roasted cauliflower with pomegranate arils. Mixing tahini, honey, and red wine vinegar creates the perfect sweet and salty combination to enhance just about anything you can think of.

¼ cup tahini

¼ cup water

Juice of 1 lemon

1 tablespoon honey

1 tablespoon red wine vinegar

In a medium bowl, combine the tahini, water, and lemon juice. Add the honey and red wine vinegar to the bowl and mix well.

Variation Tip: If you like things spicy, swap out the red wine vinegar for hot sauce!

Per serving (2 tablespoons): Calories: 109; Total fat: 8g; Total carbs: 8g; Fiber: 2g; Sugar: 5g; Protein: 3g; Sodium: 20mg

Creamy Dill Sauce

P PAREVE **G** GLUTEN FREE **GF** GRAIN FREE **◯** NUT FREE **SF** SUGAR FREE **V** VEGETARIAN

MAKES ABOUT ½ CUP | PREP TIME: 5 MINUTES

I am all about the sauce. Some things are only as good as what you dip them in, and this creamy dill sauce is an example of how just a few ingredients can create a really delicious addition to just about anything. A few dishes that are especially tasty with this sauce are Fried Gefilte Fish Patties (page 66) and crispy salmon nuggets. This is also fantastic served over spiced baked salmon.

½ cup mayonnaise

1 tablespoon freshly chopped dill

½ teaspoon freshly ground black pepper

¼ teaspoon salt

Juice of 1 lemon

In a medium bowl, combine the mayonnaise, dill, pepper, salt, and lemon juice until smooth and well combined.

Variation Tip: Add 1 or 2 crushed garlic cloves to enhance the flavor.

Per serving (2 tablespoons): Calories: 185; Total fat: 20g; Total carbs: 1g; Fiber: 0g; Sugar: 0g; Protein: 0g; Sodium: 331mg

Creamy Nacho Sauce

D DAIRY **NUT FREE** **SF** SUGAR FREE **V** VEGETARIAN

MAKES ABOUT 2 CUPS | PREP TIME: 5 MINUTES | COOK TIME: 10 MINUTES

It is not a plate of nachos unless it is smothered under a thick layer of rich, creamy Cheddar sauce. My pet peeve is restaurant nachos that are nothing more than tortilla chips with a few strips of cheese melted on top. I want to get in the kitchen and show them how easy it is to make this creamy Cheddar sauce.

2 tablespoons butter

2 tablespoons all-purpose flour

1 cup milk

1 cup shredded Cheddar cheese

1. In a large pot over medium heat, melt the butter, then add the flour and whisk together until well combined and a paste forms.

2. Add the milk and whisk until the sauce thickens.

3. Turn off the heat, add the shredded cheese, and continue whisking until the cheese melts and the sauce is smooth.

Per serving (¼ cup): Calories: 105; Total fat: 8g; Total carbs: 3g; Fiber: 0g; Sugar: 2g; Protein: 5g; Sodium: 123mg

Pico de Gallo

P PAREVE G GLUTEN FREE GF GRAIN FREE NUT FREE SF SUGAR FREE V VEGAN

MAKES 2 CUPS | PREP TIME: 5 MINUTES

Pico de gallo is a deliciously fresh tomato salsa with chopped cilantro and onions and fresh lime juice. Jalapeños are a punchy addition, but they are optional if you want to skip the spice. I love spooning this on tacos and nachos, or eating it with crispy Coconut-Crusted Tilapia (page 65) or Spiced Salmon (page 67). You can switch up the flavor by adding diced mango, peaches, or strawberries to the mix.

8 Roma tomatoes, diced

1 cup chopped fresh cilantro

1 large white onion, diced

1 jalapeño pepper, seeded and diced (optional)

Juice of 1 lime

½ teaspoon salt

In a large mixing bowl, combine the tomatoes, cilantro, onion, and jalapeño (if using) in a bowl. Add the lime juice, season with salt, and mix well.

Make-ahead Tip: While pico de gallo tastes best fresh, it can be prepared in advance and kept in the refrigerator in an airtight container for up to 3 days.

Per serving (¼ cup): Calories: 32; Total fat: 1g; Total carbs: 7g; Fiber: 2g; Sugar: 4g; Protein: 1g; Sodium: 155mg

Candied Kosher Beef "Bacon"

MEAT · **G** GLUTEN FREE · **GF** GRAIN FREE · **NUT FREE**

SERVES 4 TO 6 | PREP TIME: 5 MINUTES | COOK TIME: 15 MINUTES

While bacon is not kosher, there are many products in the kosher industry that mimic its flavor and texture using kosher turkey or beef, and these candied kosher beef strips are simply delicious. Sweet and salty with caramelized sugar, they are addictive straight from the oven (I always steal a few before serving them!), and they are even better stuffed inside challah or served over crispy potato kugel, creamy mashed potatoes, or nondairy Alfredo pasta.

¼ cup packed brown sugar

4 ounces kosher beef "bacon" or beef fry

1. Preheat the oven to 350°F. Line a baking sheet with parchment paper.

2. Rub the brown sugar over the beef "bacon" strips and place them on the prepared baking sheet. Bake for about 15 minutes or until the edges are crispy.

3. Enjoy the strips whole or cut them into bite-size pieces.

Per serving: Calories: 144; Total fat: 10g; Total carbs: 9g; Fiber: 0g; Sugar: 9g; Protein: 4g; Sodium: 280mg

Balsamic–Brown Sugar Vinaigrette

P PAREVE G GLUTEN FREE GF GRAIN FREE NUT FREE V VEGAN

MAKES ABOUT ½ CUP | PREP TIME: 5 MINUTES

I love a good, tasty salad dressing, and this balsamic–brown sugar vinaigrette is a really delicious one, featuring just the right sweetness-to-tartness ratio. It goes well over almost any salad, especially one that uses kale, spinach leaves, or arugula as a base. It pairs very nicely with fruits like apple, strawberries, or peaches. Crumbled salty feta and creamy avocado would also taste fantastic.

¼ cup extra-virgin olive oil

2 tablespoons balsamic vinegar

2 tablespoons brown sugar

In a medium mixing bowl, whisk together the olive oil, balsamic vinegar, and brown sugar until well combined.

Variation Tip: Add a clove of crushed garlic, minced shallots, a spoonful of mustard, or chopped fresh herbs. You can double the recipe and combine it in a mason jar with a lid, storing leftover vinaigrette in the refrigerator for up to a week.

Per serving (2 tablespoons): Calories: 127; Total fat: 13g; Total carbs: 5g; Fiber: 0g; Sugar: 4g; Protein: 0g; Sodium: 2mg

Tzimmes (Candied Carrots)

P PAREVE **♥** FAMILY FAVORITE **G** GLUTEN FREE **GF** GRAIN FREE **⊗** NUT FREE **V** VEGETARIAN | SERVES 4 TO 6 | PREP TIME: 10 MINUTES | COOK TIME: 1 HOUR 15 MINUTES

This tzimmes recipe is a family favorite. It was given to my mother by our neighbor and dear friend, Bella Raksin. When I think of Rosh Hashanah, Sukkot, and just about any holiday meal, these sweet candied carrots are the first thing that come to mind. I enjoy them serving them over creamy mashed potatoes or along with a serving of crispy potato kugel. The carrots add a great flavor and texture to potato-based holiday staples.

1 teaspoon cooking oil

4 to 6 carrots, peeled and cut into thin rounds

3 tablespoons honey

4 tablespoons sugar

¼ cup orange juice

Pinch salt

1. In a large saucepan, heat the oil over medium-high heat and cook the carrots for 15 minutes, until they are slightly softened, stirring occasionally so they don't stick.

2. Add the honey, sugar, orange juice, and salt to the pan. Combine well and cook over low heat for an hour, stirring every so often so the carrots don't stick to the pot.

Variation Tip: Add 2 pineapple slices (or ¼ cup pineapple chunks) and cook for an additional 10 minutes.

Per serving: Calories: 147; Total fat: 2g; Total carbs: 36g; Fiber: 2g; Sugar: 31g; Protein: 1g; Sodium: 103mg

Classic Buttercream Frosting

P PAREVE **G** GLUTEN FREE **GF** GRAIN FREE **V** VEGAN

MAKES ABOUT 3 CUPS, ENOUGH TO FROST ONE 9-BY-13-INCH CAKE OR 24 CUPCAKES

PREP TIME: 10 MINUTES

I'm a frosting-over-flowers kind of girl, which means there is no way I'm baking cupcakes without topping them with a thick layer of sweet icing. In fact, most often, I make cakes and cupcakes just so I can whip up some homemade frosting to slather on them. This is a classic, rich buttercream for any flavor cake. You can easily play around with the flavor by adding in chopped strawberries, peanut butter, lemon juice, or even cookie-butter spread.

1 stick (½ cup) margarine, at room temperature

1 (16-ounce) box powdered sugar

¼ cup almond milk or water

1 teaspoon vanilla extract

Using an electric beater, cream together the margarine, powdered sugar, milk, and vanilla. Add water or almond milk to thin the frosting, or add more powdered sugar to create a thicker frosting.

Variation Tip: Swap out margarine and use peanut butter in its place. Replace milk with lemon juice for a tart lemon frosting.

Per serving: Calories: 216; Total fat: 8g; Total carbs: 38g; Fiber: 0g; Sugar: 37g; Protein: 0g; Sodium: 90mg

HOLIDAY MENUS

MY FAVORITE MEMORIES are all food based, and they usually include delicious details of cooking and baking for all of the Jewish holidays with my mother and siblings. Each holiday has its own special food connected to it: baking cinnamon apple pie in preparation for Rosh Hashanah to symbolize a sweet and prosperous new year ahead, or frying up golden-brown latkes in oil for Hanukkah as we rejoice in the miraculous defeat of the Maccabees and the wonder of one tiny jar of oil lasting eight long nights. My very first food memory is shaping and stuffing hamantaschen with jam for Purim (see page 175 for a photo!), and I fondly recall cleaning out the kitchen for Passover and cooking gluten-free recipes like egg noodles and chocolate fudge brownies. And, of course, we welcomed Shabbat each weekend with freshly baked challah loaves and crispy-edged potato kugel, sweet noodle kugel, and chicken soup with matzo balls.

Food has always been a source of connection to me—a way of bringing people together as they sit around the table, passing dishes and sharing stories. I hope you enjoy these easy holiday menus that feature some of my favorite recipes to cook and serve throughout the year. May they bring you joy and allow you to create your own memories and traditions.

SHABBAT MENU

Friday is not meant for complicated. Erev Shabbat prep is hectic enough without the added stress of recipes that require multiple steps and pots to clean. When it comes to my own personal weekend menu, I stick with the classic tried-and-true recipes that I grew up with—most of which are super easy to prepare. The only exception to my rule of simplicity is challah. While it does require more effort than I usually like, whenever I smell the fresh scent of challah baking, I am immediately flooded with memories of watching my mother bake it on Thursday nights. Warm and crispy from the oven, it's the perfect way to welcome Shabbat.

Shabbat

Classic Hummus (page 14)

Flatbread Salad (page 17)

Kani Bites with Creamy Dill Sauce (page 48)

Classic Potato Kugel (page 59)

Sweet Noodle Kugel Muffins (page 33)

Lemon Chicken with Rosemary and Thyme (page 76)

Strawberry Apple Crumble (page 131)

ROSH HASHANAH MENU

Rosh Hashanah is the first holiday of the Jewish New Year. The name itself literally means "head of the year," and we celebrate the holiday by eating *simanim*, or foods that symbolize having a sweet year that is plentiful with both good deeds and good merit. Some of these foods include apples, honey, carrots, pomegranates, beets, spinach, black-eyed peas, green beans, fish, and dates. To add the most meaning to our holiday meal, we incorporate these items into as many dishes as possible.

Rosh Hashanah

Blackberry Pomegranate Spritzer (page 24)

Tilapia Baked with Cumin, Tomatoes, and Potatoes (page 84)

Tzimmes (Candied Carrots) (page 142)

Spinach Quinoa Patties (page 58)

Quinoa Salad with Avocado and Pomegranate Seeds (page 35)

Apple Cider Chicken with Apples and Pears (page 82)

Apple Pie Egg Rolls (page 119)

Cinnamon Coconut Whipped Cream (page 27)

HANUKKAH MENU

Hanukkah is the festival of lights—and all things fried and dusted with sugar. Much like children who wait for the holidays to unwrap presents, I eagerly anticipate this holiday so I can stuff myself with powdered jelly donuts and fried potato latkes.

When it comes to celebrating Hanukkah, I like to think of everyone's favorite fried food—latkes—and the exciting nontraditional ways to eat them! Whenever I'm trying to give the basic latke a makeover, I think of other potato treats, like French fries or baked potatoes. What do I enjoy topping those with, and would it work with a latke? The answer is usually yes! I've served "nacho" latkes with a creamy Cheddar sauce, poutine-inspired latkes with gravy, and even grilled-cheese latkes. To make your own creative latke recipes, think of your go-to comfort dishes, then use the components as toppings or fillings for a classic latke recipe.

Meanwhile, surprise your family by creating a holiday latke out of their favorite weekday dish and add them to these simple and delicious recipes for a Hanukkah buffet. Here are two menu options for the holiday. One is a meat-based menu—built around my Reuben–Stuffed Latkes—and one is dairy based, if you opt for a variation like the grilled-cheese latkes mentioned above (these are super simple: just place sliced mozzarella between two plain potato latkes and cook in the oven or in a pan on the stovetop until the cheese has melted).

Hanukkah

MEAT MENU:

Reuben–Stuffed Latkes
(page 36)

Easy Mimosas (page 23)

Barbecue Pastrami–Wrapped Asparagus (page 41)

Asian Coleslaw Salad
(page 22)

DAIRY MENU:

Grilled-Cheese Latkes
(see left)

Cheese Pancakes (page 72)

Oven-Roasted Tomato Soup
(page 57)

Broccoli Cheddar Bites
(page 40)

Strawberry Feta Salad
(page 16)

PURIM MENU

I adore Purim. One of the ways in which we celebrate the holiday is by making and eating hamantaschen. The three-cornered pastry is a holiday treat, traditionally filled with poppy seeds and various jams. Devouring it is symbolic of overcoming evil. Purim is a fun and festive day, and the hamantaschen we bake should reflect the joy of the holiday we celebrate. My first memories in the kitchen are of baking hamantaschen with my sisters. All nine of us would gather around the table cutting out circles of pastry dough, stuffing them with jam, shaping them into triangles, and eagerly waiting for them to be ready to bite into. Now that I am all grown up with a kitchen of my own, I enjoy making modern updates to this traditional dessert with unique and fun flavors.

Purim

Shredded Kale Salad with Creamy Tahini Dressing (page 15)

Vegetable Basmati Rice with Honey (page 38)

Spinach and Beef Stuffed Shells (page 71)

Funfetti® Hamantaschen (page 126)

Vegan Toaster Pastries (page 112; turn them into hamantaschen by cutting dough into triangles)

Hamantaschen Ice Cream Sandwiches (page 128)

SHAVUOT MENU

On Shavuot, we celebrate by eating all things dairy—from classic cheesecake to creamy pastas, from cheese-infused salads to fresh-from-the-oven strawberry cheese danishes. It's a holiday filled with dairy delights.

Shavuot

Strawberry Feta Salad (page 16)

Perfectly Creamy Mac and Cheese (page 42)

Greek-Style Stuffed Salmon (page 87)

Barbecue Cauliflower Poppers (page 55)

Classic Creamy Cheesecake (page 117)

Strawberry Cheese Danish (page 120)

PASSOVER MENU

Passover is one of my favorite holidays. It falls near my birthday, which could have something to do with it, but it's not just the cake and gifts that I look forward to. Growing up, many of my friends dreaded the holiday of no bread, but there is no need to panic on Passover. Sure, it can be difficult to go without our usual menu essentials such as rice, pasta, and gluten flour, but that doesn't mean your meal has to be limited to bland and tasteless foods. With a few easy swaps you can still enjoy year-round favorites such as chicken noodle soup and meat sauce and pasta, as well as decadent chocolate fudge brownies—all kosher for Passover!

Passover

Fried Gefilte Fish Patties (page 68)

Gluten-Free Egg "Noodles" (page 39)

Sausage Egg Muffins (page 54)

Matzo Pancakes (Brei) (page 34)

Sausage-Stuffed Sweet Potatoes (page 56)

Coconut-Crusted Tilapia (page 65)

Gluten-Free Brownie S'mores (page 130)

Passover Substitution Guide

Passover food can be really delicious. Gluten is not allowed, but with a few simple swaps there are still so many tasty ways to enjoy your favorite foods. Try a few of these strategies for adapting your go-to recipes:

- When you are missing traditional pasta over the holiday, cook spaghetti squash and zucchini noodles in place of the usual noodles. Meatballs taste fantastic served over both those options.

- Use kosher-for-Passover macaroons instead of graham crackers as a crust for cheesecake. Simply crush the macaroons and combine them with melted butter. Once baked with the creamy cheese batter layered on top, the final result tastes just as good.

- I typically serve vegetable kugel (like broccoli or spinach) in a deep-dish flaky piecrust throughout the year. For Passover, I simply skip the pie base and bake the filling in muffin pans to make individual crustless servings.

- Swap out flour for potato starch in most recipes, such as when coating schnitzel or baking brownies.

- In the end, you don't have to limit yourself to the standard, common recipes for Passover—think bigger!

Popular Kosher Symbols

Full list at https://www.kashrut.com/agencies/

Rabbinical Council of California (RCC)

3780 Wilshire Blvd #420
Los Angeles, CA 90010
(213) 389-3382
Beth Din Fax: (213) 234-4558
Kashrut Fax: (562) 286-5235

Chicago Rabbinical Council (CRC)

2701 W. Howard, Chicago, IL 60645
(773) 465-3900, Fax: (773) 465-6632
Rabbi Gedalia D. Schwartz, Av Beis Din
Rabbi R. Sholem Fishbane,
   Kashrus Administrator
E-mail: info@crcweb.org
Website: http://www.crcweb.org

The Union of Orthodox Jewish Congregations (OU)

Eleven Broadway, New York, NY 10004
(212) 563-4000, Fax: (212) 564-9054
Rabbi Menachem Genack,
   Rabbinic Administrator
Kashrus Questions Hotline:
   (212) 613-8241
E-mail: kosherq@ou.org or
   bergc@ou.org
Website: http://www.oukosher.org
New companies: birnbaum@ou.org

The Organized Kashrus Laboratories (OK)

391 Troy Ave., Brooklyn, NY 11213
(718) 756-7500, Fax: (718) 756-7503
Rabbi Don Yoel Levy,
   Kashruth Administrator
E-Mail: General: info@ok.org
Info on Certification:
   cfogelman@ok.org
Website: http://www.ok.org

"Star-K" Kosher Certification (STAR-K)

122 Slade Avenue, Suite 300
   Baltimore, MD 21208
(410) 484-4110, Fax: (410) 653-9294
Rabbi Moshe Heinemann,
   Rabbinic Administrator
Dr. Avrom Pollak, President
E-mail: star-k@star-k.org
Website: http://www.star-k.org

"KOF-K" Kosher Supervision (KOF-K)

201 The Plaza, Teaneck, NJ 07666
(201) 837-0500, Fax: (201) 837-0126
Rabbi Dr. H. Zecharia Senter,
   Executive Administrator
Rabbi Gissinger, Rabbi Kahn,
   Rabbi Katz: KOF-K bais din
E-mail: info@kof-k.org
Website: http://www.kof-k.org

Kehilla Kosher

P.O. Box 480739, Los Angeles,
   CA 90048
(323) 935-8383, Fax: 323-372-3574
Rabbi Daniel Elkouby,
   Kashrus Administrator
Rabbi Avrohom Teichman, Rabbinic
   Administrator/Rav HaMachshir
E-mail: office@kehillakosher.org
Website: http://www.kehillakosher.org

Kosher Supervision of America (KSA)

P.O. Box 35721, Los Angeles, CA 90035
(310) 282-0444, Fax: (310) 282-0505
Rabbi Binyomin Lisbon,
   Kashrus Administrator
E-mail: info@ksakosher.com
Website: http://www.ksakosher.com

Measurement Conversions

VOLUME EQUIVALENTS (LIQUID)

US STANDARD	US STANDARD (OUNCES)	METRIC (APPROXIMATE)
2 tablespoons	1 fl. oz.	30 mL
¼ cup	2 fl. oz.	60 mL
½ cup	4 fl. oz.	120 mL
1 cup	8 fl. oz.	240 mL
1½ cups	12 fl. oz.	355 mL
2 cups or 1 pint	16 fl. oz.	475 mL
4 cups or 1 quart	32 fl. oz.	1 L
1 gallon	128 fl. oz.	4 L

OVEN TEMPERATURES

FAHRENHEIT (F)	CELSIUS (C) (APPROXIMATE)
250°F	120°C
300°F	150°C
325°F	165°C
350°F	180°C
375°F	190°C
400°F	200°C
425°F	220°C
450°F	230°C

VOLUME EQUIVALENTS (DRY)

US STANDARD	METRIC (APPROXIMATE)
⅛ teaspoon	0.5 mL
¼ teaspoon	1 mL
½ teaspoon	2 mL
¾ teaspoon	4 mL
1 teaspoon	5 mL
1 tablespoon	15 mL
¼ cup	59 mL
⅓ cup	79 mL
½ cup	118 mL
⅔ cup	156 mL
¾ cup	177 mL
1 cup	235 mL
2 cups or 1 pint	475 mL
3 cups	700 mL
4 cups or 1 quart	1 L

WEIGHT EQUIVALENTS

US STANDARD	METRIC (APPROXIMATE)
½ ounce	15 g
1 ounce	30 g
2 ounces	60 g
4 ounces	115 g
8 ounces	225 g
12 ounces	340 g
16 ounces or 1 pound	455 g

Recipe Index by Meal Type

Index

Acknowledgments

To my boys, Dovi and Moshe. Your love and laughter bring such joy to my life daily. I am so proud to be your mommy. You are my favorite helpers in the kitchen and there is no one I enjoy sharing cupcakes with more.

To my mom and pops, I am forever grateful for your unwavering dedication. Thank you for raising me with the love and support that made me believe I could truly do anything. Pops, you showed me what hard work can create, and whenever I doubt myself it is your voice reminding me that I can do it. Mama, your loving faithful heart is what guides me. My love for food and the power it has to heal and connect starts with you and the home you raised me in. Thank you.

To my sisters, all eight of you: Rivky, Tova, Chanie, Mushky, Sari, Shanie, Debby, and Michal. Thank you for constantly being by my side. The joy of sisters is never feeling alone (and always having someone to share food with).

To my brothers, Shlomie and Mendy. I've only got one big brother and one little bro, and you both are the very best.

To my sisters-in-law, our mutual love for celebrating life with good food truly makes you feel like sisters. I'm thankful my brothers chose each of you, and blessed to have you in my life.

To my brothers-in-law, thank you for your continued love and support. Our family holiday table is livelier with each of you around it.

To my friends, I am grateful for each and every single one of you. Whether it is chatting over coffee, laughing over drinks, or catching up over dinner, there is no joy like sharing food with the people you love, and I cherish these moments with each one of you.

To my editor Bridget and the team that helped shape this book, thank you for being patient and guiding me throughout this process. I am deeply grateful.

Most of all, I am thankful to G-d for blessing me with this opportunity to share my passion for food with all of you.

About the Author

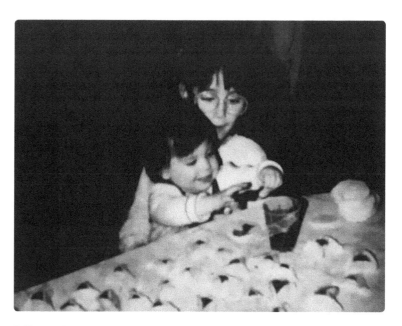

Nina Safar is a food blogger and founder of kosherinthekitch.com. She was raised in a big Brooklyn family full of love for food and tradition, and now channels that passion into cooking and sharing food that blends tradition and culture. She admits to having zero patience for difficult recipes, which is why she creates easy and convenient dishes that don't compromise on flavor. She now whips up recipes (with her two sons standing by for snacks) at her home in Los Angeles.